VICTORIA PLUMB

AGNES SZUDEK

Victoria Plumb

Illustrated by Gillian Gaze

HUTCHINSON JUNIOR BOOKS

Hutchinson Junior Books Ltd
3 Fitzroy Square, London WIP 6JD

An imprint of the Hutchinson Publishing Group

London Melbourne Sydney Auckland
Wellington Johannesburg and agencies
throughout the world

First published 1978
Text © Agnes Szudek 1978
Illustrations © Hutchinson Junior Books Ltd 1978

Set in Monotype Baskerville

Printed in Great Britain at The Anchor Press Ltd
and bound by Wm Brendon & Son Ltd
both of Tiptree, Essex

ISBN 0 09 131040 7

To
Hope Leresche

A dream's a dream until the day
One meets it face to face;
And faith may be close-linked with hope,
If Jubilee's the Place!

Contents

Victoria Plumb

Victoria Plumb was standing on her head in the corner of her bedroom. She often stood on her head. All the Plumbs did it. Grandfather Plumb said it was the surest way of living to a ripe old age, and he was old enough to know what he was talking about. Victoria stayed quite still, watching a fly on the ceiling. 'It will probably live to a ripe old age, I expect,' she muttered in an upside-down voice.

At that moment her mother called from the bottom of the stairs: 'VICTORIA?' Soapy suds plopped from her yellow rubber gloves onto the floral hall carpet, like frothy morning dew.

'Yes Mum?'

'Come down duckie. I want you to run along to the corner shop for me.'

'Coming.'

Victoria tossed her legs to the floor, and the fly shot off the ceiling in alarm. Together they left the room at top speed.

Mrs Plumb was busy writing out the shopping

list as Victoria skidded across the vinyl tiles in her socks.

'Do put your shoes on child,' she scolded. 'You'll wear out my patience, your socks and my expensive flooring with all your zig-zagging. Are you listening to me?'

'I'm all ears Mum, look,' said Victoria, pulling her ears out sideways as far as they would go.

Her mother gave her a withering look. 'Now see here, get this right for once, will you? All I want is: a large packet of noodles, one pound of green bananas – green mind you! I've got a West Indian recipe called Banana Boats I want to try out for dinner, and I want half a dozen eggs – jumbo size. Got that?'

Victoria nodded. She wasn't really listening because her mother had written it out anyway. 'Oh, yes,' she went on, 'and pop into old Harris the joiner and tell him to keep the second-hand drawers. He knows the ones I mean, with the Queen Anne legs. I'll pay him when I can get along. Now is that too much for you to remember?'

'No Mum. I'll get it right,' said Victoria who was on her head again trying to unhook her cardigan from a peg with her right foot. 'I could do more than that, if you like.'

'I doubt that very much. You're a scatterbrain! That's Grandpa Plumb's upside-down business for you. Stands to reason something's bound to go wrong if you live life the wrong way up. Do try and behave like a human being before you're grown up. We're the laughing stock of Backfire Avenue.'

Although Mrs Plumb had joined the Plumbs by marrying George Plumb from the local laundry, she never considered herself to be one of them unless it was for a very good reason like cashing a postal order, or claiming a small win on the Pools.

Victoria was gone in a flash. The corner shop was no more than a hundred yards away, but it took her at least half an hour to get there – always. She stopped to stroke all the thin stray cats that stalked about or hid themselves under parked cars. She loved all those poor cats and often fed them bits of her dinner, which she secretly stuffed into her pockets at meal times whenever she could: mashed potato, a fish finger or two, scraps of meat, steamed pudding; they appreciated anything, those skinny cats. She even tried a spoonful of lobster soup one day. She knew it would be a special treat for them, but it seeped out through some loose stitching in her old school tunic, and as luck would have to have it, it trickled slowly and warmly down one of her mother's legs which was stretched out under the table. Mrs Plumb often sniffed with wonder at the tasty smells that always accompanied the washing of Victoria's school uniform, but she put them down to powerful school dinners.

As for Victoria, it was after she had played with the fourth cat and offered it a piece of her chewing gum, the only thing she had with her, that she realized she had lost the shopping list. She was still clutching the purse with the pound note inside, but the paper must have blown out of her basket.

'Columbus!' she shrieked. 'And I can't remember

a thing! I wasn't even listening!' She walked frantically back along the gutter looking among the litter that was never swept away properly, but she saw no sign of her mother's list. She sat down on the kerbstone and went through all the things she could remember having seen in Bert's shop, until at last she thought she had got it right. 'A large packet of noodles, one pound of green bananas for Banana Boats, half a dozen – what was it? Oh yes, jumbo eggs, and the drawers with the Queen Anne legs from next door.' To fix it in her mind she repeated it over and over again to the tune of 'Deckchairs Fighting In The Sky' until she reached the corner.

She put one hand up to reach the door handle of the shop, and lifted one leg to climb up the old high step, but there was no handle and no step. There was no shop on the corner at all! There was nothing but a heap of rubble from which a yellow, choking dust was still rising. As Victoria gaped, not knowing what to think, the dust cleared slightly, and there on the ground close beside her she saw a notice like a road repair sign which read:

DEMON DEMOLITION GANG
Guaranteed to reduce your home to rubble in ten
tantalising ticks.
No lines. No telephones. No communication.
Don't find us, we'll find you.

Victoria had no difficulty in reading the notice but she didn't understand what it all meant. She didn't have to wonder for long though, because as the dust cleared completely there emerged standing on top of the rubble that had once been the corner shop, the Demon Demolition Gang itself. Three tough-looking men munching hot dogs with lashings of onions stood there showing mouths full of gigantic teeth and chins full of stubble like screw nails, and all this horror was surrounded by wild black wiry hair. Victoria quaked as she looked up at them. She fairly rattled in her skin as those great mouths opened wide like loader-shovels, ready to swallow her up in one bite with the onions. But they did not eat her. Their hot dogs seemed to satisfy them well enough. Nor did they take the slightest notice of the little girl standing on the cracked pavement. They snorted and snuffed and puffed by way

of conversation with each other, wiped their greasy chins on their cuffs noisily like sandpaper on wood, then lurched away over the rubble and out of sight.

Victoria didn't know what to do for the second time that morning. Her mother was always angry if she went home without having done the shopping correctly, but things had never been as bad as this before. How could she do the shopping if the shop wasn't there? It had been there an hour before. She knew because she had been perched up on the gate-post and had seen Crombie the Crusty Baker's van stopping to deliver the bread. She liked to watch for the van every Saturday morning. The baker balanced big wooden trays of loaves and buns on top of his head as he carried them into the shop. Victoria was waiting for the day when he would drop one of the trays and give all the cats a good breakfast, but it never happened. This thought gave her an idea.

'Perhaps I'll find something that's been left behind, if I look hard enough,' she muttered. 'A noodle or two maybe, or a couple of cracked eggs – jumbo size or not. Anything will do to stop Mum from getting into one of her bulging, red-in-the-face tempers.'

She clambered about, slithering and tripping over loose bricks and plaster, pulling aside whatever she could. But, there was nothing worth picking up, nor was there the least sign of Harris's joinery shop, which had been next door. Her heart sank as she thought of returning home without having done anything she was asked. As she looked helplessly this way and that, she saw something moving out of the corner of her eye; a kind of a – thing!

She turned to look. A creature was walking up and down the pavement carrying a sandwich-board, but whether it was man, moose or maggot, Victoria Plumb had no way of telling. The thing wore outsize furry boots, a purple and brown sleeping suit like the kind babies wear, a bright yellow bolero simply riddled with pockets, and an assortment of hats on its head rising up like a challenge to gravity. The black and white sandwich-board bore letters in bold red ink:

THE RAPID RESTORER

BUILDINGS A SPECIALITY
WHAT'S COME DOWN, CAN GO UP
THE PROOF OF THE PUDDING'S IN THE
EATING

Since there was no one about, and the little striped thing went on walking rapidly up and down just in front of her, Victoria thought it must be trying to attract her attention.

'Er – excuse me, Sir, Madam, or to whom it may concern,' she ventured, not knowing how to address the creature. 'I'm looking for the shop that used to be here – Bert's actually.'

Immediately the creature stopped abruptly, turned its head to look at her then manoeuvred over sideways and spoke: 'I thought you would require me sooner or later young lady. I always follow in the wake of the Demon Demolition Gang. It is my duty. Like pilot fish with sharks, or tick birds with cattle. You may go where you wish, but I go where I must, and as my board says: "The proof of the pudding's in the eating"!' The creature wrapped one arm around the front of the sandwich-board, pointing to the sentence.

'But why not say the proof of the *sandwich* is in the eating,' said Victoria, who had taken an instant liking to the fellow. She felt safe now in thinking of him as a fellow instead of a thing. He had a kind little face with round wide-awake eyes like a bush-baby. 'After all,' she went on, 'it is a sandwich-board you're carrying.'

'Ah, but that would be dangerous Miss Plumb. Someone might think *I* am the sandwich and take a bite out of me. No thank you, I'm safer with pudding.'

'How did you know my name?' asked Victoria sharply.

'You told me.'

'No I didn't. Not a word of it, honestly!' replied Victoria correctly.

'In that case I must be thinking ahead again. It's a bad habit and I really must stop it. It seems to upset people. Talking of heads, it's time for business, Miss Plumb. If it's Bert's shop you want, it's Bert's shop you will have.'

He crouched on the ground so that his sandwich-board touched the pavement, then neatly crept out of it without knocking off any of his hats. Very skilfully he pulled his trouser pockets inside out to show that there was nothing in them, and did a little heel-and-toe dance with his eyes tightly shut.

The furry boots waved and flapped as though they were alive.

'It would help no end if you could possibly stand on your head Miss P.,' he said breathlessly. 'But – but – I suppose that's too much to expect.'

'Not Pea – it's Plumb! And, yes I can! Oh, I can do that better than anything else in the world!' squealed Victoria throwing herself into a somersault. She had no wall to lean against since Bert's shop was gone, but she managed to stand upside-down as straight as a rod. She too kept her eyes closed, but not to help the Rapid Restorer; rather for fear some of the neighbours might walk by, especially Mrs McKnocker from next door who knew everybody's business and none of her own. They all thought the Plumbs were half potty already and she knew she would be in terrible trouble if her mother heard she had been living 'the wrong way up' on the public footpath. But strangely enough the street was deserted as though everyone had fled or hidden in terror from the Demon Demolition Gang.

In a moment the heel-and-toe dance stopped. '*Voilà!* as they say in the Common Market,' announced the Rapid Restorer. 'It's not quite as it used to be, but it's good enough. Let's go in.'

Victoria opened her eyes and stood up. Bert's shop had grown up again from the rubble, and indeed it was not at all as it had been. It just looked like rubble that had been sorted out into a square shape, with the door and window frames leaning against it.

'After you,' said the Rapid Restorer, who was in fact something of a gentleman. Victoria walked inside, past the door which he held up in his arms. It was very dark until the little fellow produced a jar full of glow-worms from one of his bolero pockets. There was just enough light for two, and none to spare. 'At your service. Can I help you?' he asked, sounding just like Bert.

Victoria was so startled by all that had happened to her that she couldn't remember what her mother wanted. She hummed: 'Deckchairs Fighting In The Sky', but that didn't help. 'Corks! I can't think. I've no idea,' she said, feeling stupid.

'But my dear Miss Plumb. Have you put me to all this trouble for nothing? Surely not. Think hard before the DDGs return and knock us down.'

'The who?'

'The DDGs. They'll be on the job again in a minute. Do think, Miss Plumb. Harder! Harder!' The Rapid Restorer was looking very alarmed.

'Oh dear, I am silly . . .' began Victoria. 'But wait – I think, I think it was something like this: a large packet of poodles, six banana boats, half a dozen eggs with Queen Anne legs and . . . and . . . there was something else from next door. Yes, I know, the second-hand drawers, jumbo size. Mum said she'll pay for them later. That's it – I hope.' She had trotted it all out so quickly she hardly knew what she had said.

'Say no more,' said the Rapid Restorer with relief. 'We've just managed it in time. Steady your legs, the earth's shaking.' They both felt the ground shudder under their feet. The DDGs were coming back to finish the job. 'Hurry along now, Miss Plumb,' said the little fellow, pushing Victoria towards the doorway. 'We'll meet again, no doubt. Your entire district is going to be demolished soon, so I won't be far away.'

'Thank you very much,' said Victoria gratefully. 'You'll find me any day on the gatepost. You're my best friend, Mr Rapid Restorer.'

'Oh, one more word, Miss Plumb. Does your mother make pancakes?'

'Yes, good ones, on Pancake Tuesday.'

'With currants?' he begged, with hands joined fervently.

'Loads!' replied Victoria.

'In that case we're friends forever, Miss Plumb. My nose can smell a pancake cooking light years away. Now be off.'

'But, I nearly forgot, where's the shopping?' gasped Victoria, with one leg already out on the pavement.

'Here we are. Just pull these two strings along and the shopping will follow. It's better to pull than to push, and it's better to pull than to carry. The proof of the pudding's in the eating, remember.'

Victoria pulled on the strings that had been thrust into her hands. As she leapt clear of the building, there was a deafening crash, and Bert's shop had gone again in a cloud of yellow dust. She didn't wait for it to settle. Dragging what felt like a ton weight behind her, she didn't stop or look back until she reached the garden gate. Her mother was waiting on the porch, and looking angry – her bulging red-in-the-face anger.

'Where you been – Krakatoa?' she yelled, using one of the few place names she knew east of the Suez Canal, on account of its famous volcano. But her voice trailed away in a fainting scream: 'EEEEEeeeeek!' as she collapsed on the doorstep.

Victoria turned round and saw what she had been pulling home. Precisely what she had asked for in the shop! There were: six banana boats freshly in from Jamaica, full of the greenest-looking bananas she had ever seen. In front of them stood half a dozen eggs on sturdy, well polished Queen Anne legs, an outrageous pair of outsize winter drawers, very second-hand by the look of the patches, and a huge packet, which at that very moment burst open to reveal dozens of noisy, yapping poodles.

The poodles immediately spotted the stray cats and chased them down Backfire Avenue until they all disappeared from sight. The eggs marched off in formation like a well trained army in the direction of Lavender Hill, with the outsize drawers flapping along like a regimental flag; while from the six banana boats came forth the smooth, oily sound of a steel band playing 'The Banana Boat Song', and they sailed away with their cargo over a dark sea of tarmac.

Victoria stood with her eyes and mouth wide open. She was horrified and completely bewildered. 'It's my head,' she murmured. 'I'll unscrew it and have it pickled the right way up.'

Just then Mrs McKnocker from next door came rushing out to see what all the commotion was about. Most of it she had already seen from behind the curtain. She looked a treat with her head full of plastic curlers, and one eye heavily made-up in orange and green.

'Whatever's wrong?' she squawked. Then she saw Mrs Plumb lying full stretch across the flower border with her head among the white alyssum. ' 'Sakes, it's Mrs Plumb! She's gone. Dead as a duck, and my Sidney's in the bath. SID – NEY? Quick, come down. Mrs Plumb's gone! Get the fire brigade!' She screeched this at the top of her voice, then rushed back into the house.

That's when Victoria came to her senses. Of course her mother wasn't as dead as a duck, or any other kind of fowl. She had only passed out, not passed on.

Victoria ran into the kitchen and brought out a cup of water. She held it to her mother's head until she opened her eyes and took a drink. 'Ooooh, my head! Don't know what came over me. Must have been one of my weak turns. Quite got me, it did. Help me into the house Victoria, I'm making an exhibition of myself.'

Mrs McKnocker came running out again carrying a ladder for a stretcher, with her husband Sidney behind her in his bare feet and rolled in a bath towel. 'Oh look, she's not dead after all,' cried Mrs McKnocker in a dismayed kind of voice, dropping the ladder which she no longer needed. 'Don't worry, Mrs Plumb,' she said. 'It must have been the shock of seeing all those poodles leaping out of a packet, and the six banana boats.'

'I should say so, definitely,' added Mr McKnocker, 'to say nothing of half a dozen eggs on Queen Anne legs and great blooming patched-up drawers that went off in the wind!'

Mrs Plumb's eyes narrowed to slits. She opened and closed her mouth several times like a fish, but said nothing. Then, swiftly she drew Victoria into the house and slammed the front door. 'How dare they ever again say the Plumbs are potty! How dare they ever have said it in the first place? They're lunatics! Raving lunatics, racing about half dressed telling me I'm dead. And what was the ladder for may I ask? To help me up to heaven no doubt. And all that gibberish about. . . .'

Just then her eyes alighted on the shopping that was on the kitchen table: one large packet of noodles, half a dozen eggs – jumbo size, one pound of green bananas, and on the floor beside them was a second-hand set of drawers with Queen Anne legs. The very one she wanted.

'Victoria, what a good girl you are. You're the cleverest Plumb in Christendom. About your head my pet, you have my permission to stand on it whenever you like. There might be something in it after all that you can teach the world.'

Victoria smiled, and her smile became wider and wider as she saw the top of a sandwich-board and a tower of assorted hats scuttling away past the kitchen window.

The Crash Landing

After the disappearance of Bert's corner shop, and Harris the joiner, life was much duller in Backfire Avenue. But it did mean that Victoria had a little further to go on errands for her mother, so she did see more of life, in a kind of a way. Whole terraces of houses were being pulled down, for better things to be put up, she was told. Looting and Sockwell seemed to be choked with left-overs, after the Demon Demolition Gang had been around. With the light of dawn, extraordinary things were seen on the pavements, in the gutters and up alley-ways. Sometimes whole three-piece suites, bedsteads and cookers were all out in the open, looking for new homes. 'At least they don't need feeding, not like the stray cats under the cars,' thought Victoria.

One day she found a perfectly clean old drawer, lined with green felt which she took home and filled with note books, pencils and crayons. She kept it neatly under her bed, together with other neatly kept things. Another day she spotted six very old tiles, from a fireplace, patterned with beautiful orange lilies. She spread these out on her window-sill, like a flower garden. But her mother did not like the new interest at all.

'What you think you're doing, my girl, bringing all this stuff home? As if we haven't got a house full of rubbish already. There's your father's old chair with its springs showing like Mrs McKnocker's curlers, and here you are, collecting enough junk to start a market.'

She said this several times over a number of weeks. But, it was on the day that Victoria brought home an old-fashioned pram, with the rubber gone from its wheels, that Mrs Plumb really became angry. She was in the kitchen, plucking leaves off a lettuce, and complaining about the greenflies in the sink, when Victoria peeped round the kitchen door.

The cold tap was running noisily, so Victoria sneaked the pram into the kitchen behind her mother, and out through the other door into the hall. She was hoping to get it up to her bedroom without being seen. She was about three-quarters of the way upstairs, drawing the pram gently over each step, when her mother came into the hall. She gaped, with her mouth open wide enough to fall off her face, before she squealed: 'VIC – TORIAAA! What ARE you doing? Have you gone completely mad? Where's that thing going? And, where did it come from?'

'A rubbish dump. Oh, Mum, it's my special treasure,' groaned Victoria. 'Can't I have it in my room with me? Please.'

Mrs Plumb uttered no words, only opened and

closed her mouth like a fish, as she always did when she thought she was shocked. Then she began to climb the stairs, stamping, as though she was leading an army on the attack.

Victoria stood still. Until that moment, her idea had not seemed unreasonable. Her mother had almost reached her when the door-bell rang. Like the Grand Old Duke of York, Mrs Plumb was neither up nor down, so she tramped round on one step until she made up her mind that she ought to see who was at the door. Away she marched, down to the hall and jerked open the front door.

A red-faced man in dungarees stood on the porch step. 'Fine stable manure for your garden, missus?' he said, jovially. 'Your flowers look as if they could do with a good feed.'

Mrs Plumb was absolutely livid: 'Well I – well, of all the – that's all I need, I'm sure, some manure to add to everything else the Plumbs collect. Kindly take your horse and cart away from my premises, my good man, or I'll call the health inspector. You've got all the flies in Sockwell buzzing round your cart, apart from what's in my sink. It's not hygienic!'

'Sorry, missus. Didn't mean to pollute you,' said the man, clearly surprised at the hostile reception. 'Just thought you'd like a bit of manure, that's all.'

'Goodbye,' said Mrs Plumb, closing the door. She stood in the hall, trying to remember what she had been doing before. 'Where was I. . . ? Oh, yes, the salad,' she muttered, and went back to her lettuce, forgetting about the pram, which by this time was in Victoria's room, covered with her pink quilt.

Now, having safely brought it up, Victoria thought of several reasons why the pram would be better at ground level. She knew she couldn't possibly manoeuvre it up and down the stairs every day. 'I wonder,' she murmured. 'Maybe I could rig up a pulley outside the window, and lower the pram that way, then Mum wouldn't notice.'

Excitedly she opened her wardrobe door and pounced upon: one yard of French knitting, some plastic strips and odd bits of crochet cotton. There wasn't enough of anything to reach down to the garden, but anyway she began by joining all the pieces together. Then she knotted on several pairs of socks and winter tights, and finally she added her new school scarf. She wrapped one end of her rope around the pram, secured it with a good knot, and tied the other end to the leg of her bed.

Gently, gently, she eased the pram out over the windowsill, and by gradually playing out the rope, the pram began to swing downwards into the garden. But it was at that moment she heard her mother's voice below in the garden.

'Well, would you believe it! Forty pence for half a pound, and I paid forty-two! Sauce I call it! I've got a good mind to take it back only we're having macaroni cheese for tea, and it's not the same without the cheese.'

Mrs Plumb was holding a piece of cheddar cheese in her hand and complaining across the fence to Mrs McKnocker who was holding a similar piece.

'It's all because of that Eurovision Common Market, dear,' went on Mrs Plumb. 'Not right at all. I'd rather have my own market and buy my cheese at the right price.'

Just then a dark shadow loomed over them, and at the same time an aircraft roared overhead.

'LOOK OUT, MRS PLUMB! A jumbo jet! It's coming down on top of us,' screamed Mrs McKnocker.

Both women threw themselves face downwards on the soil. Mrs Plumb lay tightly pressed against a bed of spring onions, while Mrs McKnocker, on her side of the fence, was crushing a well-ripened strawberry patch. They lay still, waiting for an explosion, but nothing happened. The sound of the aircraft faded away. Mrs Plumb bravely opened one eye and looked up.

The thing was still there, but it was certainly not a jumbo jet. It was swaying about, and coming lower and lower. Mrs Plumb raised herself on her elbows: 'A PRAM! A pram – in the air! VIC – TORIAAAA?' She sprang to her feet, forgetting all about the piece of cheese, which by then looked like welsh-rarebit in the dark Sockwell soil. 'That child's getting the better of me,' she called to Mrs McKnocker, who was still on the ground. 'She's all Plumb, of course. Victoria? Explain yourself, d'you hear?' She banged her way upstairs to investigate.

Victoria was standing beside her bed with the end of her school scarf now round her wrist. 'Sorry Mum,' she said. 'I thought I'd move it without bothering you.'

'What ARE you doing with your new school scarf?' asked her mother. 'It took me months of hard work to knit that, now put it away at once.'

'But Mum.'

'At once, I said. This minute, you ungrateful girl.'

Victoria could see there was no point in arguing, so she unwrapped the scarf. As she did so, it flew out of her hand and shot away over the windowsill. A second later there was a horrifying crash as the pram hurtled downwards and struck the metal dustbin in the back garden. There was an unearthly howl, or something like that from Mrs McKnocker, and Mrs Plumb, with one furious glare at Victoria, marched off to conduct a further investigation.

The pram was still in one rusty piece, but a fine row of crisp Webb lettuces was flattened among potato peelings and all the usual things that can spill from dustbins.

'Well, that's got rid of the greenfly,' joked Victoria looking out of the window, but her mother appeared and shouted up: 'I'll give you three minutes, Madam, to get this contraption out of my sight, and I wonder what your father's going to say when he sees his best Webbs gone. Come here and pick up this rubbish!'

Victoria was red in the face as she came down and set about clearing up the garden. Her mother and Mrs McKnocker stared at her silently with crossed arms and legs. She was relieved when she had put the last baked bean tin in the dustbin. Then, without a glance in her mother's direction, she grasped the handle of the pram and fled at top speed.

She was almost in tears at the thought of parting with her new treasure. 'It would have been so useful,' she muttered, as she went into the glorious dump. There was such a lot she had wanted to do with the pram, and as she looked about, she saw a heap of things piled up in the middle of an old tyre; things she had actually been thinking about. She became so excited she exclaimed loudly:

'Cor!! I could make one of the wonders of the world, I could! I know I could!' She was down on her knees in a flash, picking up all kinds of objects. There was a windscreen-wiper, car side-mirrors, a broken radio aerial, oh, just about everything she could possibly want. It was almost as though they had been put there especially for her. As she tossed them one after another into the bottom of the pram, another thought occurred to her.

'Mum said to take the contraption back to the dump, didn't she? So, I have. Mum said I can't have it at home, didn't she? So, I won't. But did she say I have to abandon it?'

A sharp little voice from somewhere said: 'Certainly not!' Victoria believed it was her conscience speaking louder than usual. 'Then that settles it,' she cried triumphantly, and she threw her arms around the battered vehicle. 'I won't abandon you – ever! I'll keep you and look after you always, I promise. And since you'll be neither one thing nor another by the time I've finished with you, I'll give you a new name. You'll be a –

a pushpam. That's right, a pushpam! Nobody else has got one of those.'

She went on talking to herself. She often did. When her head was full of ideas, they just had to tumble out. And as she talked, she walked about, looking for a place to hide the pushpam.

Over in a corner, by an assortment of odd car seats, she saw what looked like a very ancient boiler, so ancient, she thought it could have come from grand, grand, grandpa Plumb's laundry. It seemed to be the best hiding place, because the boiler would probably never be moved. There she parked the pushpam, and she even saw a torn tarpaulin on a mountain of Coke tins. She dragged the tarpaulin down the mountain with a noise that could probably be heard at Land's End, but she didn't care. Her mind was on something else.

'What I've got to have, before my pushpam takes to the high road, is an L plate,' she said jokingly. 'I wonder where I could. . . .' She swung round on her heel, and saw – an L plate propped up on one of the car seats. She hadn't noticed it before, but there it was. Just what she wanted. It looked strangely new, or at least freshly wiped over. She put it into the pushpam and covered the whole lot with the tarpaulin, perfectly.

It had taken her so long to do this, she was afraid her mother might think she had run away from home. 'If I know Mum, she'll have Looting and Sockwell turned inside-out for me,' she murmured. It was time to take her leave.

Standing well back from her little heap of

treasure, she raised her arms and uttered a grand and fond farewell:

'It is a far, far better thing that I do, than I have ever done; and still obeyed my mother, Mrs Plumb.'

The first part was something her father always announced when he was particularly pleased with himself; a piece from Charles Dickens he said. The last piece was Victoria Plumb. The performance left her feeling so tearful, she pulled her hanky from her pocket. As she dabbed her eyes, she felt she was doing it with a baked bean. She was! It must have slipped into her pocket following the crash-landing in the back garden. Hoping it had been no further than the maker's tin and her pocket, she popped the bean into her mouth, and started to run. She did her best school sprint in her best school plimsolls. How she raced! Smoke seemed to rise from her rubbers as she singed along to Backfire Avenue.

By the time she got there, she thought she was dying of thirst and nearly fell into the kitchen sink as she turned on the tap.

'Well, did you get rid of that awful thing, Victoria?' asked her mother, who was ironing at the kitchen table.

'Y-y-yes, Mum. It's back in the rubbish dump,' gulped Victoria.

'Where it belongs,' said Mrs Plumb, pressing her lips and the iron at the same time. 'Whatever is the matter with you now? You'll drown in all that water you're drinking. What's wrong, girl?'

'Nothing much really, Mum. I think it was that

one baked bean I ate on the way home, not to mention the half-minute mile I ran at the same time.'

'One baked bean? Half-minute mile?' echoed Mrs Plumb.

'Mmm. The bean was in my pocket, so I ate it. The bean, not the pocket,' replied Victoria. Then she wished she had said nothing at all.

Mrs Plumb looked at first as though she was going to be shocked, but changed her mind and said soothingly: 'Go and lie down until tea-time, there's a good girl. You must have a fever coming on.'

Victoria went to her room and lay down on her bed happily until tea-time, without a fever, but with her head full of marvellous ideas for the treasured pushpam which she knew would be hers for ever and ever.

Victoria Goes to Town

During the next few weeks, Victoria spent much of her time half-way under her bed, where she kept her green drawer. She was working out plans for her pushpam, sketching it and jotting down every idea that came into her head. It was, after all, going to be one of the wonders of the world. But she did not get back to see it as soon as she had expected.

Mrs Plumb always had things lined up for her to do at weekends, like shopping, and more shopping, or cleaning out a corner, or a cupboard. As Mr Plumb said: 'She's always on the go, your Mum. Never stops.'

The next 'go' was early Christmas shopping. Mrs Plumb decided to do it extra early, because that's what the big stores were doing. She knew this from television. 'It seems to me it gets earlier every year,' she said. 'We'll have Santa Claus crunching along the beach at Brighton next summer, if you ask me.' She was always saying things which indeed no one would ever have thought of asking her.

Loaded with bags and baskets, Mrs Plumb and Victoria walked to their shopping centre, and found that the local department store had closed down. 'But it can't have,' said Mrs Plumb defiantly. 'I bought a pair of tights there only last week, I think, and nobody said anything about closing down. I was born and bred here, and I'm the last one to know what's going on. What a cheek!'

Cheek or not, the huge department store was completely empty. The doors were bolted and red notices were plastered all over the windows.

Victoria was as disappointed as her mother, but it was not long before she had an idea. 'I know Mum! Let's go to town. Come on, just for once. All the stores in London can't have shut down.'

'Well, I . . . Well, I . . .' Mrs Plumb was numb with shock as Victoria steered her across the road to the underground station.

'Let's go to Parrots. Somebody once told me they've got everything there, even a zoo! Be a sport, Mum, be a sport!'

Mrs Plumb couldn't think of being a sport or anything beyond those great red stickers on her store, so, absent-mindedly, she let Victoria get the tickets. Away they went on the new Victoria Line, which, for obvious reasons, Victoria regarded as her very own. They had to change trains, naturally. Nothing is ever as easy as it seems, if you want to live life excitingly, and by the time Mrs Plumb and her daughter walked into the scented warmth of Parrots department store, Victoria was thrilled to the marrow.

'Oh, Mum, are we really here?' she gasped, twisting her scarf into a string.

'Don't go strangling yourself, Victoria. Of course we're here. It says so. And what's more, don't go asking for everything you set eyes on, my girl, else you'll end up with nothing in your stocking, Christmas morning.' Mrs Plumb fingered the labels on everything she passed, and pursed her lips together as she made a mental note of pounds and pence.

They went up in the lift to the toy department, and for an hour Victoria stared, wide-eyed at the display. There were stuffed toys, the size of giants, games she had never even heard of, mechanical toys with bells that rang, tanks that fired, dogs that barked for their dinner; while overhead, toy birds swooped about all on their own, fluttering their brilliant wings.

But what surprised Victoria most of all was that children could touch anything they liked. Flutes, saxophones, trumpets, drums and goodness knows what, were blown and banged, and nobody seemed to mind. It was not at all like Snuffs, her local bookshop, where she had once been told to clear off for looking through a comic she had been going to buy anyway.

Mrs Plumb couldn't find a chair to sit on, because there wasn't one, so she sat on an upturned box, looking with glazed eyes, as though she was in a dream. There was even a self-service toy section with wire baskets, just like her own Co-op. She came to her senses when Victoria tried to pull her towards the baskets.

'No, thank you, Victoria. If you go in there you've

got to buy something, else they'll think you've hidden it somewhere. I'm not going.'

'Please,' begged Victoria. 'Just a packet of balloons, that's all. I'll buy it with my own pocket money. Look, I've got it with me.'

This satisfied her mother, and with her rare purchase of assorted balloons in a small plastic bag, Victoria felt as proud as if she had bought the whole shop.

A stroke of either good or bad luck always seems to be around the corner at Christmas time – even early Christmas time. So it was for Victoria that day. As she came out of Parrots, dazzled by the wonder of all she had seen, she slipped head-first into the gutter. On the way down, her forehead struck the lamp of an enormous car that was parked by the kerb. One of Parrots' doormen, a giant of a man, was holding open a padded leather door for a stately-looking lady and gentleman who were about to step in. As Victoria looked up from the ground, large snowflakes began to fall, and she had a vision of an elephant's trunk bending very close to her, and a voice saying:

'The poor lamb! She's cut her head. Silly old lamp. Now what shall we do?'

The next moment, in a buzz of adults all talking at once, Victoria felt strong arms holding her as the doorman lifted her into the huge car. Her mother was with her, and two elephants, she thought. But when they drove off, her head began to clear and she saw that one of the elephants was the grand old lady she had just seen by the shop,

and the other elephant was an old gentleman who seemed to be miles away in front at the steering wheel.

'No need to worry,' he called over his shoulder. 'We'll be back to barracks in no time and have you patched up as good as new.'

'Yes, yes, my lamb,' said the old lady, patting Victoria's knee. 'We'll have a cup of tea, and find a sticking-plaster for that poor head.'

Mrs Plumb introduced herself, and nearly fell off her seat when she learned in return that she was in the presence of Sir Partridge and Lady Dragora Dowser. She was so overcome with surprise that for the third time that day, she had nothing to say.

The Dowsers were in fact ancient nobility. Sir Partridge was ninety-two years old, and was sure he could remember seeing the Spanish Armada approaching Plymouth Sound. Most people agreed that his well-used memory was playing tricks on him, but he *might* have had a relative who was bowling with Sir Francis Drake on that historic day in 1588. Lady Dragora was also very old. So was their car, a First Choice Roaster, or FCR model. It occupied three parking meters at the same time, and brought confusion to the minds of traffic wardens. The Dowsers also had a very long dining table at home. They sat one at either end and talked to each other like yodellers across a valley, until the day Sir Partridge found a piece of piping that someone had thrown away. He took it home and hung it from the ceiling, over the dining table, longways. When Lady Dragora saw it, she said:

'How ghastly!' And it became known as the ghast pipe. She grew to like it though, when she found how easily they could whisper down it to each other, and it added a touch of excitement to their meals. It was the pride and joy of Sir Partridge's old age.

Such was the life of the Dowsers in whose car Mrs Plumb sat so unexpectedly, and oh, so silently.

'We haven't far to go, only round to Eatwell Place,' said Lady Dragora, and Victoria noticed in the fading light how the pearls round the old lady's neck swung from left to right as she spoke, while her nose, like a counter-balance went up and down, up and down.

A few moments later they were turning towards a row of white, expensive houses, looking as carefully preserved as a jar of pickled cucumbers. Sir Partridge was just about to halt, when they came to a gap in the row, so he revved the engine and drove on, only to splutter to a stop and reverse until he came again to the gap in the row of houses

'Dragora, do you see what I see?' he asked, fixing on an eyeglass from a black ribbon round his neck.

'Well, I don't see number forty-three, if that's what you mean,' answered Lady Dragora, pressing her face to the window.

It was true. Their house, number forty-three, had gone. It had been demolished! Its crumbled remains lay sprawled untidily open to a square of darkening sky from which the first evening star twinkled down.

Sir Partridge was the first to recover. 'It's those dashed Spaniards!' he cried waving his fists. 'Told

41

you time and time again I saw the Armada coming, Draggy. But you wouldn't believe me.'

'Whoever did it my love, it certainly wasn't the Armada, I assure you . . .' began Lady Dragora.

'Assure me – rubbish!' retorted Sir Partridge. 'The whole place reeks of onions. Isn't that enough for you?'

Mrs Plumb felt drowned in all this information. She had heard about the Spanish Armada when she was at school long ago, so if the Spaniards had done it once, there was no reason why they shouldn't try it again, she thought. 'Mmm, 'tis a bit smelly,' was all the help she could offer. 'Give me Backfire Avenue any day.'

They clambered out of the car and surveyed the damage. It reminded Victoria of the day Bert's corner shop had been demolished; the day she met the Rapid Restorer. She recalled that when they parted, he had promised to visit her regularly for currant pancakes, but she hadn't seen him for some months.

Sir Partridge and Lady Dragora were climbing about the rubble of their home, looking greatly distressed, when suddenly Victoria had a brilliant idea. 'Mum?' she asked, urgently. 'When's Pancake Tuesday?'

'Pancake Tues – Victoria, don't be tiresome. You know very well it's on a Tuesday. Those poor dears. What a catastrophe!' She was watching the Dowsers who had seized with glee the only remaining objects they could find in one piece – the dining-table and the ghast pipe.

'But WHICH Tuesday?' persisted Victoria.

Her mother looked at her in exasperation, as though she was going to have one of her red-in-the-face bouts of anger. But Mrs Plumb remembered just in time about Victoria's knock on the head, so she smoothed away her frown. 'I'm not sure,' she said quietly. 'But I'll find out when we get home, if it's all that important to you.'

Sir Partridge and Lady Dragora, bedraggled and covered with dust, were staggering back to the pavement with their table.

'I'll just trot back for the ghast pipe Draggy,' he panted. 'Life wouldn't be the same without it, eh?' And back he went into the ruins to retrieve his one and only invention, his conversation piece.

'So sorry to be inhospitable like this,' said Lady Dragora trying to remain dignified in spite of her trembling knees. 'But who could have imagined having no home to come back to! Nobody told us we were due to be demolished. It just goes to show, you can't tell what's going to happen next.'

'Lucky thing we went out Dragora, or we might have been demolished too.' Sir Partridge was coming back dragging the ghast pipe that banged and clattered like an old tin can. 'And without so much as a "by your leave", the dashed villains.'

'It's a diabolical liberty, dear,' said Mrs Plumb, gently, being of the opinion that it is polite to call everybody 'dear'.

Lady Dragora smiled kindly, and turned to her husband. 'What to do now Partridge? We've brought this little girl and her mother here for nothing. There's not even a bit of sticking-plaster left to offer them.'

'I'm sure I don't know,' said Sir Partridge, peering through his ghast pipe. He had forgotten all about Victoria's head. 'Can't see a thing through this, you know – not a thing!' he snorted. It was not surprising. The other end of the ghast pipe was against his trouser-leg.

It was Mrs Plumb who made the most sensible suggestion. 'Well, it's been nice meeting you. We'll go and catch the train home. Must get Victoria to bed. Good night, all.' She was about to hustle Victoria away, when Lady Dragora said:

'No, no, Mrs Plumb. If my husband can pull himself together, we'll drive you home. It's the very least we can do. Isn't it my angel?'

'Yes, we can't do more – I mean we can't do less. It's the absolute least – oh, let's get in. I say, who's going to drive? Can you Mrs Plumb?'

'No use looking at me, your reverence. The Hoover's my vehicle,' said Mrs Plumb, who couldn't even ride a bicycle.

'Splendid! Splendid! Let's take the Hoover. Convenient, is it?' asked Sir Partridge looking about him.

Mrs Plumb shot him a look of mixed feelings: was he making a fool of her, or was he as potty as the McKnockers, her next-door neighbours? She wasn't clever enough to know which, but Victoria shrieked with unladylike laughter and went hopping up and down the pavement.

What happened in the end was that they all

climbed into the spacious First Choice Roaster and settled themselves comfortably with travelling rugs over their knees like royalty; then they all piled out again on to the pavement, opened up the double doors in the middle of the vehicle and pushed in the dining table and the ghast pipe. Sir Partridge had an idea that they might both be gone before they got back again.

At last the curious assembly set off at a swinging angle all over the road, and headed vaguely in the direction of Vauxhall Bridge, from where they hoped to reach the Plumbs' home. Lady Dragora was the one who was not too hopeful because she knew Sir Partridge's sense of direction was as weak as his eyesight.

After what seemed like hours they at last reached Vauxhall Bridge where everything was chaos and clutter with road works. Abandoned cranes, loaders and dump trucks stood about like monstrous watch-dogs, and worst of all, the traffic lights were out of order. Sir Partridge had no difficulty whatever in losing the main road and bumping up over some wooden planking on to an unfinished road extension. The going was so rough that the excellent suspension of the First Choice Roaster was hardly noticeable.

It was while they were jogging over a wide, desolate expanse like No-man's-land in the shadowy night that they heard a weird wailing in the distance. The stately Dragora began to wilt for the first time that day. Her pearls seemed to droop and her lace dress to crumple. 'Oh Partridge, where are we?' she called out bitterly down the ghast pipe. But all she received in reply was a mumble, which she couldn't understand.

'Mrs Plumb, are you sure this is the right direction?' she asked, anxiously.

'I've not the faintest, dear,' replied Mrs Plumb. 'Now I could tell you if we were underground, but above ground, I'm lost.'

Victoria, who had been straining her ears to try and distinguish the strange sounds on the night air, suddenly called out: 'Ssssh! Listen! Can't you hear?'

They rolled down the windows and listened. They could hear singing of a kind, but not the Vauxhall Choral Society, although the melody was familiar.

'It must be the hereafter,' sighed Lady Dragora resignedly, for she was a religious woman at heart; and it seemed to her by the bleak panoramic view from the windows that they had reached the end of the world.

'Sounds more like "John Brown's Body" if you ask me,' said Mrs Plumb sulkily. She was not too pleased to hear that her vicinity looked like a dead end.

The boisterous solo coming through the ghast pipe was certainly Sir Partridge singing 'John Brown's Body', but the singing coming through the windows had different words altogether. Quite distinctly they heard:

'We'll whisk away your ceiling and we'll whisk away your walls,
We'll whisk away your banisters until your staircase falls;
We'll smash up all your chandeliers and wreck your marble halls,
Then we'll all go marching home.

46

We're the demolition gangsters, the dreaded demolition gangsters,
Double rubble trouble gangsters,
Now we're off to spend a quiet night at home.'

'I knew it,' squealed Victoria. 'It's the Demon Demolition Gang. I thought it looked like their work in Eatwell Place, and it smelt like it too.'

Mrs Plumb and Lady Dragora exchanged knowing looks, as if to say: 'The accident to her head was worse than we thought.' They persuaded Victoria to lie flat for the rest of the journey, and she actually fell asleep. It had after all been a very busy and exciting day.

Somehow or other, Sir Partridge managed to reach Backfire Avenue and occupied the full length of it with his First Choice Roaster. There was no question of his and Lady Dragora's driving back to town that night; in fact they had nothing to go back to, so Mrs Plumb invited them to stay overnight in the spare bedroom. They gratefully accepted, and after a superb supper of toasted cheese crumpets, they went to bed happily, feeling as though they were in a five star hotel.

Victoria had a bad night. She dreamt about the Demon Demolition Gang and woke up several times screaming for currant pancakes. Mrs Plumb, after crawling out of bed for the fourth time in her bare feet (she had lent her slippers to Lady Dragora), assured her daughter that it was Pancake Tuesday THE VERY NEXT DAY! She knew it wasn't, of course. Well, it couldn't be, not the week before Christmas, but it seemed to be what Victoria wanted to hear.

47

'There now,' she said, stroking Victoria's forehead. 'We'll have a kitchen full of pancakes, black with currants, if only you'll go to sleep like a decent Christian!' Victoria was already asleep, smiling contentedly.

The next day, the pretend Pancake Tuesday, Mrs Plumb behaved like Supreme Champion at Crufts. She was queen of all she surveyed, almost dribbling with enthusiasm at having nobility in the house, and a First Choice Roaster in the avenue for everyone to see. 'SIR PARTRIDGE' and 'LADY DRAGORA' were shrieked at full throttle, fit to burst the ancient eardrums of her two elderly guests.

The McKnockers next door took that very day to dig their garden, the part nearest the Plumbs. Mrs McKnocker had never laid a finger on the garden before, but there she was in her fur-trimmed slippers, shifting soil about with her husband Sidney. And, so intent were they upon listening to every word from the Plumbs' household, that they sliced the heads off their very late-flowering chrysanthemums, without even noticing.

Mrs Plumb's greatest regret was that her husband George was not at home to share her triumph. His laundry had lost two pairs of her folk-weave curtains, and he vowed he would not return home until he found them. He was a very conscientious worker, Mr Plumb.

Victoria spent the morning standing on her head on the gatepost. The Dowsers thought it was a charming display for their benefit, but Victoria was really watching out for the Rapid Restorer. He came of course as she knew he would when the smell of currant pancakes rose in the air and floated beyond the borders of Looting and Sockwell. She saw his hats coming from afar down Lavender Hill, and she went to meet him, walking on her hands.

It wasn't long before the Rapid Restorer had parked his sandwich-board alongside the First Choice Roaster and joined everyone in the front parlour. Mrs Plumb was so beside herself with joy that she noticed nothing odd in the little fellow who wore wild furry boots, a striped stretch suit, not to mention the tower of hats on his head. As for the Dowsers, perhaps they thought it was the fashion south of the river.

As they ate their way through mountains of pancakes, Sir Partridge and Lady Dragora told the sad tale of their house in Eatwell Place. The Rapid Restorer promised to help, which was really what the pretend Pancake Tuesday was all about.

Mrs Plumb put on her best flower-petal hat, and they were all about to leave when Mr Plumb arrived beaming, and flourishing two pairs of curtains. 'Found them, Mrs P!! Found them like I said,' he called.

'Oh, what adorable folk-weaves!' cried Lady Dragora. So Mrs Plumb very generously gave them to her, because she didn't really care for them herself, and wouldn't have minded if she had never seen them again.

Then away they all went, driving dangerously

back to Eatwell Place, leaving Mr Plumb to finish off what was left of the pancakes.

In the daylight, Vauxhall Bridge chaos did not look quite so much like the hereafter, and they arrived safely at SW1.

They stood in a circle on the pavement while the Rapid Restorer pulled his pockets inside-out and did a little heel-and-toe dance, with his eyes tightly

shut. At the same time, he implored Victoria to stand on her head. As she did so, number forty-three rose up from the rubble, brick by brick, and once again took its place in the row of houses, as neat as a pickled cucumber.

Everyone clapped and shouted: 'HOORAY! HOORAY!'

'Three cheers for Victoria Plumb and the Rapid

Restorer,' cried Sir Partridge down the ghast pipe, which he was holding like an alpine horn.

'Three cheers for currant pancakes!' called the faint voice of the Rapid Restorer, as he scurried away in the direction of Drone Square.

'How extraordinarily well everything has turned out!' said Lady Dragora, clasping her hands with joy.

'Yes, down and out and up again, by billyo,' chuckled Sir Partridge, already dragging the ghast pipe into the house. Between them, they managed to get the dining table inside, because although it was very long, it was fortunately, very narrow.

Hundreds of thank yous and goodbyes seemed to be ringing in Mrs Plumb's ears as she and Victoria went home on the underground. Mrs Plumb was quiet again. It had been two days of sudden silences for her. All she could see were those horrid red stickers all over her department store.

'You never know what's going to be round the next corner in life, do you?' was the only remark she made as the train rumbled towards Looting and Sockwell.

A Bit of Old Rome

Victoria did not forget about her pushpam. How could she, after her promise to it, forever fixed in her memory with a baked bean? Her father often wondered why she asked him frequently for nails, nuts and bolts, coach screws and other such things. He didn't ask the reason, but was pleased to think that little girls were being taught carpentry at school if that was what they liked doing. He gave her all she asked for.

Victoria rushed back and forth between her home and the ancient boiler in the rubbish dump, behind which she had hidden her pushpam. She could do anything she really set her mind to, Victoria Plumb, and before long with all its bits and pieces added, her vehicle DID look like one of the wonders of the world.

The first day she brought her mother's shopping home in it, her legs were shaking, just a little. But when Mrs Plumb saw how much shopping it could hold, she forgot she hadn't wanted it around in the first place, and had probably forgotten all about the crash landing. She wondered why Victoria didn't keep it at home, but so long as it turned up when it was needed, she was satisfied. Victoria preferred to keep it behind the boiler, because her mother so often changed her mind about things.

One day, Victoria wheeled her pushpam to the church hall, with some cast-off clothing for the jumble sale. She was taking three well-washed jumpers, four pairs of white socks, coloured somehow with indelible school paint, and a navy-blue raincoat that was too small for her. Her mother had also sent along a hand-painted vase as fine as an egg-shell which Mrs Plumb said looked like foreign junk.

The lady in the hall gave Victoria two banana toffee bars in return, so with a feeling of a job well done, Victoria went prancing along the pavement, taking the long way home. She wanted to keep out of her mother's way for a while because Mrs Plumb was cleaning the bedrooms, and there was always a row about the things she found under Victoria's bed.

The long way home was near the river. Just near enough anyway to smell the water. She could hear the ships' horns in the distance and imagine the dark grey water lapping against the barges. She thought she would look for something, to occupy the time. This was a game she often played with herself, and it was surprising the number of times something did seem to turn up.

Holding the handle of her pushpam with one hand, she jumped into all the squares of the pavement taking care not to land on the lines. She leapt on up and down for about fifteen minutes without finding anything, when all at once she felt something crunching under the front wheels. She had actually jumped on the thing before she saw what it was. Neatly folded up into a square was a thick newspaper. Victoria picked it up and read the title:

'Worm's Eye View. Never heard of it,' she muttered, aware only of the newspaper her father took for the sports page. Then she noticed the price at the top. 'Thirty pence! Wow! It's worth a fortune! I'll have to find out whose it is,' she exclaimed. It was worth a fortune to Victoria who got a penny now and again when she went on errands. Beside the price was part of an address written in pencil: 2 Rock Cres. She didn't know where that could be but she supposed it was somewhere near. There was no one in sight to ask, so she walked on hoping to meet a policeman. No sooner had she refolded the paper into its neat shape and put it in her pushpam, when she heard a sound like growling. There, on the other side of the road, as though he must have popped up from a manhole, was a boy of about eight. He was walking along sullenly wheeling a trolley filled with laundry in a plastic bag. He was pushing it well ahead of himself at arm's length as though he hoped no one would think it was with him. At the same time he told everyone who cared to listen, that it was his by saying: 'Why should I have to go to the launderette? Ain't my job. Cissy's work, that's wot.'

'Yoo-hoo! Excuse me,' called Victoria politely.

'Wot for? Wot ju want?' he shouted rudely, not having noticed her at first.

'Please, do you know Rock Cres? Is it near here?'

The boy eyed her for a moment with his head on one side: 'No, ain't never 'eard of rock cress. Tell you wot you like about rock salmon, rock buns, rock cakes, but who knows or cares about rock cress!'

'Well then,' persisted Victoria. 'Since you're so clever, perhaps you know something about Worm's Eye View. I've got. . . .' As she bent down to get the newspaper out, a pebble went zinging across the back of her right leg.

'Rock cress and worm's eye view! And wot's that you're pushing, Noah's Ark? G'wan 'op it! You're nuts,' yelled the boy. 'Clear off before the dogs get ya.'

Victoria felt her eyes filling up with hot tears. She knew there was plenty of rudeness in the world, but she hadn't often met it like this. She pressed her lips tightly together to stop herself from crying loudly and walked on, not daring to look across the road again. She tucked her head down, half expecting something else to be fired at her, but nothing came except the same voice, but not quite so rude as before:

''Ere, arf a minute. Listen!' shouted the boy. 'You take this lot to the bag-wash and I'll keep a look out for your rock cress. Scrumper Flint's the name. Wot ja say, eh?'

'I've got nothing more to say whatever,' replied

Victoria, tossing her pigtails behind her shoulders, and her short-lived tears took off in the wind. 'I'll do my own looking thank you.'

Although her tummy told her it was lunchtime, the Worm's Eye View seemed much more important so she walked on, away from the direction of her home. She read the names of all the side streets and cul-de-sacs she passed until her legs were tired and her mouth was dry. She heard the chimes of an ice-cream van in the distance and that made her more thirsty than ever.

She had just decided that she dare not go any further in case she couldn't find her way home again when she saw an old blue van set back off the road on some waste land, and written across the side of it in white paint were the words: TEA STALL. 'I might get a drink of water there,' she thought, and she walked over the dusty, grassless space of ground to the van that stood alone like a little blue oasis.

An elderly gentleman was standing drinking tea from a mug. He leaned well forward so that the dribbles would not run down his tweed suit. Instead they fell now and again on the long knitted scarf which was wound about his neck and almost reached the ground. He was slowly turning in circles as he drank, and had his back to Victoria as she parked her pushpam. The counter was very high above her and Victoria couldn't see if there was anyone in the van or not. So, she cleared her throat and called in a thin, nervous voice: 'Er, please, please may I . . . is it allowed. . . .' At once the elderly gentleman swung round and peered at her through thick grey eyebrows like frosted twigs. His nose was still in the mug. At the same time a face beamed down at her from the counter. It was light brown, with the darkest eyes she had ever seen. Great pools of black treacle they were, and on top of this midnight appearance was arranged a pale pink turban, as beautiful as the sky at dawn.

'Hameed's tea? You like some, yes?'

'Yes – no, thank you,' said Victoria. 'I wondered – I wondered if I could just have a cup of water, that's all. But please, only if I don't have to pay for it.'

'Water? Plenty water. No charge for water,' smiled Hameed kindly, showing magnificent white teeth. 'Water as free and flowing as the River Ganges.'

'Great little thing you've got there,' said the elderly gentleman, pointing to the pushpam with a fistful of sandwich. 'It runs on water does it?'

'Not likely,' replied Victoria, who had a sense of humour. 'I'm the one that's running on water, but not always. I just haven't got a bean for a cup of tea.' The smell of tea was so good that she closed her eyes and sniffed deeply.

The old gentleman smiled. 'Have a cup on me young lady. It's the best tea you'll find anywhere. Take one every day myself when I'm not off on a dig. Hameed, a cup of tea for Miss . . . Miss. . . .'

'Plumb. Victoria Plumb.'

'Victoria Plumb! What a sun-ripened name. Exquisite! Exquisite! Diggery Downside – Professor. Pleased to make your acquaintance.' He offered the small finger of his right hand, the only one he could spare from the mug he was holding. No more than the last joint of the finger was visible

because even on such a hot day he was wearing woollen mittens. Victoria shook the little finger and asked:

'Please sir, what's a dig?'

'A dig? Why it's a dig of course. You know, archaeology – digging up the past.'

'Oh that's it. ARCHAEOLOGY!' squealed Victoria so excitedly that Hameed's eyes rolled like marbles as he handed her a mug of tea. '2 Rock Cres. and Worm's Eye View. Does that mean anything to you?'

'Most decidedly. I live at number 2 Rockery Crescent and I take the Worm's Eye View newspaper every month. I've got a copy in my pocket.'

'No you haven't! I've got it!' said Victoria diving into the pushpam. 'I found it on the pavement, and I've been looking for the owner ever since.'

'Oh my dear girl, how kind of you. There are so few of these printed I might never have got another copy. How can I reward you? Would you like a bun? All little girls like buns, don't they?'

'I don't know about all little girls, but elephants do,' said Victoria.

'Why so they do. Have you got one?'

'What, a bun?'

'No, an elephant.'

'ELEPHANT? 'Course not! My Mum won't even let me keep a stray cat. Why, do I look like a circus girl or something?' By this time, Hameed had given Victoria an iced bun.

'Well, not this way up, and yet I have a feeling I've seen you performing somewhere.'

'Upside-down on my gatepost?' suggested Victoria. 'Backfire Avenue, that's where I live.'

'Of course! The delightful fairy on the gatepost. You know, I was good at that sort of thing when I was young.' The professor put his mug on the counter, unhooked a cane from his arm, which had been under his scarf, and swished it about as though he was going to break into a dance. But, as the cane was poised upwards, the professor glared at the top of the van.

'Something on top of your van Hameed. What is it?' he asked.

'I don't know. Maybe a cat.'

'By ginger! It's not a cat! It's a hat! An odd-looking pointed thing too,' cried the professor. 'The wind must have blown it up. I'll give it a swipe with my stick.' He made a lunge and struck at the hat, but it didn't budge. Victoria ran back a few paces until she could just see it, and she knew at once by the shape that it was the top of a pile of hats, and she knew who was underneath.

'Can't move the wretched thing – must be cemented, and I've lost me puff,' gasped Professor Downside.

'Well, maybe it's on somebody's head,' ventured Victoria, not wanting to give her friend away.

'What? As high as that? Shouldn't think so, unless it's a giant.' But when the professor looked up again, the hat had moved further along the van. 'Ah, there it goes,' he called excitedly. 'I'll get it this time. Smack it square on if I can.' But although he smacked away as hard as he could, the hat did

not move. 'Something fishy here,' he said in exasperation. 'Keep still my girl, I'll investigate.'

As he hurried round the back of the van, the
Rapid Restorer moved round to the front and came
over to Victoria, sideways: 'Dear Miss Plumb, we
meet again. This time by accident, and without
pancakes. That gentleman is determined to destroy
my tip-top hat, but he'll break his walking-stick
before he so much as creases it.'

'He's very nice really,' whispered Victoria. 'He
didn't know it was on somebody's head.'

Hameed was busy buttering bread. He could not
see the Rapid Restorer who was keeping well out of
sight. In the meantime, the professor was almost
shaking the life out of a tree behind the van, thinking
that was where the hat must have blown. He came
shuffling back slowly, and the Rapid Restorer slunk
away sideways to hide again behind the van.

'Can't figure it out,' panted the professor. 'I must
be dreaming. And, d'you know, I dropped the rest
of my cheese sandwich in the – well, I'll be toasted!
It's there again.' He turned, and with a new burst of
energy flew again to the attack behind the van.

'No, no please don't hurt him, he's my friend,'
shouted Victoria, afraid that little Rapid Restorer
would be flattened in the assault. But there was no
danger. Professor Diggery Downside was standing
with his mouth wide open, and the Rapid Restorer
was staring back at him with a huge grin.

'What in the world . . .? What is it? Who are
you?' inquired the professor.

'He's my Rapid Restorer,' gulped Victoria,

skidding to a halt beside her little friend. 'We work together. Our enemies are the Demon Demolition Gang.'

Professor Downside began to read from the sandwich-board: ' "What's come down, can go up. The proof of the pudding's in the eating." Do I understand you are a restorer of buildings?' His eyes lit up with pleasure as the Rapid Restorer nodded his head vigorously. 'Oh, I'm so glad I lost my newspaper and met you. We could do with a regiment of Rapid Restorers nowadays. The country's going to bits and pieces, tumbling down about our ears. We'll all be buried up to our elbows in rubble before long if it goes on. Are there any more like you?' he asked hopefully.

'Sad to say, no. Not quite. I wander alone. Go where I must.'

'My dear fellow. You are most interesting. Do you live near here?'

The Rapid Restorer looked behind him as though to make sure no one else was listening: 'Albert Bridge. Underneath. Secret door. No visitors allowed,' he said in a whisper.

'Quite so,' said the professor softly. 'And can you restore any building you like?'

'Almost, or thereabouts. I do my best work after currant pancakes, and I must have something to work on. A freshly demolished building is what I like best of all. I must have proof that something has been there before I can restore it, if you follow me.'

'Oh, perfectly, perfectly,' said the professor,

tapping his cheek as if swift thoughts were forming in his mind. He walked up and down twirling his stick, then stopped smartly in front of the Rapid Restorer: 'Forgive my boldness sir, but would you do something for me? A job of restoration?'

'Always ready to help,' said the little fellow. 'So, your house has been knocked down?'

'No, not MY house. Someone else's house, and it's buried, not demolished.' The Rapid Restorer was beginning to shake his head, so Victoria whispered to the Professor: 'Offer him a pancake.'

'Let me offer you a pancake,' said Professor Downside loudly. 'Step this way please.' They walked round to the counter, but the Rapid Restorer didn't look happy. 'It's not my line at all,' he said. 'It could be dangerous. I might lose all my powers. But the proof of the pudding's in the eating. Tell me about it.' He put his sandwich-board on the ground and stepped out of it without disturbing any of his hats.

Hameed's eyes stretched open to their limit when he saw his new customer. He held out a plate piled high with pancakes, and each one coated thickly with butter like little moonscapes.

'It's like this,' the professor began. 'There's an old house nearby that's due to be pulled down any day, and under it I believe we will find a great treasure – a well preserved Roman villa of a very special kind. I heard about it from my father long ago, and I've waited all my life for a chance to find it.'

'You want to start digging when the house is demolished, is that it Professor?' asked Victoria.

'Precisely. I've asked the council to give me time to arrange a dig, but they've refused. A multi-storey car park is to be put up in double-quick time, so I'm told,' sighed the professor.

'Clearly a race against time and the DDGs,' said the Rapid Restorer. 'They specialize in double-quick rubble trouble. We'll have to work fast.' He pushed the remaining three pancakes into the pockets of his yellow bolero without seeming to mind at all about the greasy butter, then he crept into his sandwich-board, lifted it up and said: 'Show me the quickest way.'

'Bravo! Follow me,' shouted Professor Downside, waving his walking stick in the air like a sword and striding away over the dusty ground.

Victoria wasn't sure what to do. She thought perhaps she ought to go home. She knew her mother would be wondering what had happened to her. She could imagine her darting out of the house to take a quick look along the avenue, while the eggs got cold and the toast turned black. But how could she miss one of her friend's clever tricks? Who would do a head-stand for him? The professor was too old for acrobatics. So, without thinking further about her lunch, she grabbed her pushpam and went rattling away after Diggery Downside and the Rapid Restorer who were well ahead, and already turning into a tree-lined street.

'Thanks for the water, Hameed. See you again,' she called over her shoulder. The puzzled Indian had come out of his van, and was standing shaking his head. 'Meaningless behaviour! Such meaningless behaviour!' he muttered.

Meanwhile the professor was racing along in high spirits with the Rapid Restorer running as hard as he could on his little legs. Victoria zoomed after them, scooping her pushpam around corners on two wheels, and above the sound of her rackety vehicle she could hear the droning of an engine. It was the Demon Demolition Gang working at top speed. As Victoria came round the last bend she saw a once beautiful white house crumbling in a thunderous battle. A loader truck was hurtling a long beam of masonry against the walls of the house, which was falling apart like a set of building bricks. The loader reversed and charged again, throwing its heavy weapon into the battle until the entire house was gradually flattened.

Professor Downside watched from behind a tree, with his long scarf protecting his face from the dust. The Rapid Restorer was crouching inside his sandwich-board. Only his round eyes and column of hats could be seen. The dry dust swirling about was enough to choke a stick as Victoria joined them. She kicked the foot-brake on, climbed into the pushpam and pulled up the hood. Smartly she knotted her pigtails under her nose, but her legs, which were too long to fit inside the vehicle, had to hang down outside.

All three kept still and silent. Victoria was almost lulled to sleep by the droning of the loader's engine. When it stopped abruptly, the sudden silence woke

65

her up. She jerked so sharply that the pushpam tilted down on its handle and she slid out onto the ground. As she sat in the dust, frozen with fear, a voice like thunder rumbled by: 'Knock it off Fruity. I've had enough of this.' It was the driver of the loader, rocking the earth as his big boots hit the ground.

'Oh no, he can't!' Victoria cried and she clasped her hands over her head, thinking it was that which was going to be knocked off.

'Right you are Tosher, I could do with a bite,' said another voice. 'PLONKER?' he roared to a third man who was not in sight. 'Break, mate!'

From somewhere among the rubble emerged Plonker, as fierce looking as the other two. Victoria recognized them as the three who had demolished her corner shop, only now their screw-nail beards had grown and sprouted out in all directions. They did not seem to know they were being watched, and marched away in step loud enough for a battalion, singing as they went:

'We'll whisk away your ceiling and we'll whisk away your walls,
We'll whisk away your banisters until your staircase falls;
We'll smash up all your chandeliers and wreck your marble halls,
Then we'll all go marching home.'

As the Demon Demolition Gang faded in the distance, Victoria, Professor and the Rapid Restorer came to life, all talking at once. 'Where shall we . . .? Do you know . . .? No time to lose. . . .' until the professor waved his hat for silence.

'Don't let's get carried away dear friends,' he

began. 'Now is our only moment to try your skill, Mr Rapid Restorer. Are you ready?'

'Ever ready and always,' declared the little man licking his fingers. Victoria could see at once by the empty pockets that he had just finished off the pancakes and was about to begin. 'Miss Plumb, is your head in good order? This is a tricky one. Here we go.' He pulled his trouser pockets inside-out, closed his eyes and began his little heel-and-toe dance while his furry boots shivered and shook like wild animals.

Victoria was in great form, standing to attention on her head. 'Of course,' whispered the professor to himself, 'that's the child from the gatepost and no mistake.' Apart from this remark he said nothing more, but stared hard at the Rapid Restorer with a faint smile on his lips as though he didn't believe anything magical could possibly happen. Nor could he have seen anything happen, for the spot

in which the Roman villa was actually rising at that moment was – behind him!!

Up it came shaking the dust of centuries from its roof, almost washing itself clean in the hot twentieth-century sunshine. It was the most perfect luxury Roman villa imaginable. Its colours were brilliant, all red, green and yellow, the walls were painted with magnificent flowering trees filled with birds. It was supported on marble columns that seemed to be touched with gold, a completely breathtaking sight.

'*Voilà*,' declared the Rapid Restorer opening his eyes widely, surprised that the trick had really worked.

The professor turned round slowly: 'It's – I can't believe it's true. In all my active life I've never seen anything like it. Why, we're actually back in Roman times.' As he was exclaiming, he was throwing off several things, one after the other. Away went his walking-stick, hat, scarf, mittens and tweed jacket. Very timidly he walked over to the villa on his toes, and hesitated before stepping inside, as though he thought it might fall apart.

'Don't worry, it's as safe as houses,' said the Rapid Restorer, encouragingly. 'Do go in, and you too Miss Plumb.'

Victoria, who was by then the right way up, tiptoed behind Professor Downside. But they had hardly set foot inside when they felt the floor vibrating, as though an army was approaching. It was the Demon Demolition Gang returning in a horrible fury. They stopped a few feet away, each one pretending to roll up his shirt sleeves, which were already rolled up.

' 'Ere, 'ere, what's up?' grunted Plonker.

'Never saw that fing 'afore,' snivelled Tosher.

'Well it won't be 'ere long lads,' snarled Fruity, diving for his loader like an Olympic swimmer.

'But gentlemen, gentlemen, this is a superb Roman villa,' cried Professor Downside, collapsing on his knees beside one of the marble pillars.

'Then take it back to Rome where it belongs 'afore I splinter it,' replied Fruity, revving his engine. But he didn't have time to get it in gear before the Rapid Restorer came to the rescue. He turned his sandwich-board inside out and printed on it in chalk:

PRESERVATION ORDER

by order,

RR

The Demolition Gang cowered when they saw it. This was the kind of notice they dreaded most of all. 'So, it's you is it?' said Plonker roughly. 'You're always following us about. A proper nuisance you are. And who's RR when he's at home?'

'Royal Regulation,' squeaked Victoria with her usual quick wit. 'Not to mention Royal Row if you dare to touch that house.'

The gang huddled together for a minute, took a swift decision, and without another word, stamped off the way they had come.

A few minutes later back they came, riding on the

footplate of the mayor's car. The mayor had been opening a special fun-fair and race-track for old age pensioners. He looked splendid in his chain and robes.

'There they are gov! That's the mob. Arrest them!' shouted the DDGs.

But the mayor beamed broadly and clasped the professor's hand. 'Diggery my old chum, it's good to see you,' he said.

'Why Norbert, I mean Mr Mayor. Bless my hat, how wonderful you look.'

'You're incredible, Diggery, as always,' went on the mayor. 'What, dug all this up in the lunch hour? You're a wizard.'

'No, no, Berty, not I. My friend here is the wizard, he . . . why he's gone! He didn't even wait for me to thank him.' There was no sign of the Rapid Restorer or his sandwich-board anywhere on the horizon.

'He never waits for thanks,' said Victoria. 'He always goes off like the wind. But I'll be in touch if you ever want him again. I ought to go now too. My Mum will be ever so worried.'

'I don't know how to thank you Miss Plumb,' said the professor.

'If you really want to thank me, please take me on a dig one day,' said Victoria, slipping off the footbrake of her pushpam.

'Capital! I'll call on you one day when I'm passing Backfire Avenue. Good-bye, dear child, good-bye.'

Victoria said good-bye, and even shook hands

with the mayor before running off to find her way home.

The Demon Demolition Gang stood glumly by, their faces twisted with fury because their double-quick rubble job had failed. They slung their denim jackets over their shoulders and shuffled away, grumbling into their chewing gum.

The grand Roman villa was allowed to stay. The local council saw that it was of more use to them than a new multi-storey car park. Plants, trees, and even fountains were arranged around it, and it was open to the public for the rest of the season. It was such a success that as far as I know, it is there still.

You could see it I suppose if you are lucky enough to stray into that elusive but charming part of London situated snugly between the regions of Looting and Sockwell.

The Runaway Tea Stall

Victoria began to save up all her pocket money to spend at Hameed's tea stall whenever she could. Her mother said she had never heard of a child with such a craving for tea, but she did not complain much. She thought it was better than eating sweets, and if it kept the child's mind off standing upside-down on the gatepost, then Mrs Plumb believed it was well worth giving her daughter an extra two pence a week, so she did.

It was not really the tea of course that Victoria wanted. She was always hoping to meet Professor Diggery Downside again. She was longing to dig up some history with him, and she knew he would keep his promise if only she could meet him again. Every Saturday she ran all the way to the tea stall. It took her nearly half an hour to reach the dusty piece of land almost at the back of Vauxhall Bridge chaos where she remembered driving one night months before. She had worn out two pairs of plimsolls so far on her Saturday trots without once meeting her professor. Neither had Hameed seen him for at least three weeks.

One Saturday, near the end of July and just before the school holidays, she stuck a little note on her gatepost. It read: 'Gone for a cup of Indian tea.' And beside this she had drawn a turban shape in pink crayon. She knew if the professor passed by he would understand where to find her.

But when she arrived at the usual place, the tea stall had gone. She knew she was in the right place by the tyre marks in the dust and the scattered cigarette ends, but the van was not to be seen. In fact there was nothing to see but heaps of yellow dust and rubble. 'Must be like living in the desert,' Victoria thought to herself. It was all so quiet and still. Suddenly she remembered the Demon Demolition Gang. She didn't want to meet them on her own – ever; especially after the business of the Roman villa. She raced towards a half demolished wall that stood all by itself a few yards away attached to nothing but the ground, and as she swerved round it with her heart thumping, she saw beyond the wall in the distance, Hameed's tea stall! It was standing on the old sloping road that led down to a rag and bone yard. She was now no longer alone in the desert, but back among the familiar rubble of good old London.

Hameed spotted her and waved his tea-towel.

'Why did you move?' shouted Victoria. 'I thought I'd never find you.'

'Greetings Victoria,' said Hameed softly. He never raised his voice. 'I had to move, for the build-

73

ers. They're going to start work over there, so I was towed here with a piece of rope. But it is such meaningless parking. See, everything slopes down, down, down!'

'Oooh yes, all your cups and things. That's not fair, is it?' said Victoria, looking at the lop-sided plates of sandwiches and buns.

'Never mind,' smiled Hameed pleasantly, showing his beautiful teeth. 'Always we are told what to do. Now, you like a cup of sloping Indian tea, yes?'

Victoria nodded and handed up a penny. Hameed never took more than a penny from her, although sometimes he refilled her mug. As she was drinking, Victoria shaded her eyes with her hand and looked into the distance.

'You still looking for the professor may be? Very strange silence. Very big mystery,' said Hameed solemnly.

'Mm, perhaps he's had an accident,' suggested Victoria.

'Oh dear yes. He's fallen into one of his digs and can't get out,' said Hameed, who knew nothing about archaeology.

'I should think he's gone abroad to Egypt or Rome, or somewhere like that,' replied Victoria. She was peering at a small figure which approached through a shimmering haze sent up from the hot ground.

'So, someone comes to our oasis,' muttered Hameed, wiping a mug and spoon in readiness.

'I wonder – could it be him? No, it's too small,' said Victoria disappointedly. 'It's one of your other regulars I expect.' Hameed didn't know who it was, and it was Victoria herself who then recognized the figure. 'Oh, no,' she groaned. 'It's that rude boy I met a few weeks ago.'

'Which boy?' asked Hameed.

'His name's Splint or Squint or something,' said Victoria, watching intently to see if he was going to throw stones at her legs again. 'I don't really know him, but he's horribly rude.'

The boy was making clouds of dust rise from his feet by deliberately flicking his toes into the ground, so that he seemed to be riding in a very slow steam engine. He went on doing this with his hands sunk deeply in his jeans pockets until he came right up to the tea stall. Abruptly he called out in a deafening roar: 'WOTCHER!!' And he seemed to expect some kind of reply.

Victoria turned away from him. She didn't want to be rude in return, but she had no idea what to say, and it didn't occur to her that he had come to see her. She had her mug of tea lifted up to her face, when a not-too-clean and heavily freckled face loomed over her shoulder.

'Mornin' Your 'ighness. Out on a little trot-about then?' he said, a little more politely.

Victoria kept the mug up to her face to avoid speaking.

'Scrumper Flint. Remember me?'

'Summmmmmmr Flinnnnn. Yummm,' answered Victoria with an echoing mumble inside her mug.

'Not an 'ard name to remember, and as mad as a pot into the bargain,' said the boy.

'Mad as a what?' asked Victoria, lowering the mug in surprise.

'Pot.'

'That's a bit odd.'

'I don't care,' said Scrumper, looking down his nose.

'Everybody says I'm mad. Suits me!'

'I wouldn't have thought it suited anybody.'

'Well, I get away wiv anyfink, see? Nobody takes any notice of me.'

'I took notice of you,' said Victoria.

'Yes, but that's because you're as mad as a pot too, ain't ya? We ought to be friends, you and me. Wot ja say?'

'I might consider it if you stop saying "ain't ya". Your speech is appalling!' Victoria said this exactly like her school teacher.

'Oh, carrots! You consider then while I swallow a cup of tea,' said Scrumper, jingling what sounded like hoards of money in his pockets. He banged a five-penny piece down on the counter as though he hoped to split it in half. Hameed did not smile at him. Scrumper turned again to Victoria. 'Right then, Your Ladyship, are we friends?' he demanded, as if he would not take 'no' for an answer.

'Well, you see, you're so – oh, no! no!' Victoria squealed as she turned to put her empty mug on the counter. The counter was slowly moving away! The van was moving away! Slowly and silently it was rolling down the hill to the cobblestones of the rag and bone yard.

'Quick, after it!' yelled Scrumper, taking off like

a bullet. Hameed was hanging over the side wailing: 'HELP! I cannot drive! I cannot drive! SAVE ME!'

Scrumper tried desperately to overtake the van, but he couldn't. He had almost reached the back wheel when a horse and cart came round the corner at the bottom of the hill and began to turn into the yard.

'STOP!' shouted Scrumper. But neither the horse nor the van understood him, and before the driver realized what was happening, the cart had collided with the tea stall.

The wooden shaft of the cart broke in half; the ragman somersaulted in the air and landed on his stomach across the horse, and together they vanished into the yard at the gallop. The cart was thrown over on its side, and this brought the blue van to a halt among old pans, cookers, broken chairs and mountains of rags. The noise was deafening. Every single thing on Hameed's stall went crashing together in the collision. The mugs and plates were broken and mixed up with tomato and egg sandwiches. Buns and doughnuts lay in crumbled pieces, and all of this was gradually soaked through with spilled milk. The tea urn was not damaged, fortunately because Hameed's tea was always piping hot.

Scrumper did not pause for a moment. He leapt aboard the van and pulled at the hand-brake, but it was already full on. He waded through the debris until he reached Hameed who was lying on the floor, dazed with shock and covered with burst

77

packages of bread. 'Alright? Are you alright?' he
kept asking until Hameed nodded his head. 'Brake
linings not good. Cheap van, very old. Ooh, my
leg!' His right leg was bent under him. It looked to
Scrumper as though it was broken.

'Don't move,' he said. 'You keep still, and I'll get
the ambulance.' Away he dashed as though he were

capable of managing anything. Victoria looked after him in wonder as he ran into the rag and bone yard to find a telephone.

Victoria climbed into the van, but there was nothing she could do but clear a way for the stretcher that would come. She knew she must not try to move Hameed until his leg had been examined. Within minutes, things began to happen. Scrumper came back with the ragman who was none the worse for his joy-ride on the horse. Between them they managed to get the cart upright and toss all the things back into it. By this time the ambulance had arrived and Hameed was carefully lifted into it. Just before he was whisked away to hospital, he threw his keys to Victoria and asked her to lock up, if there was anything worth locking up.

Victoria, Scrumper and the ragman shovelled all the mangled food and crockery into a big tin bath and carried it away to the dustbin in the yard. 'Sorry about your cart,' said Scrumper.

'Oh, that's nothing. I'll soon have it mended. I'm handy at that sort of thing,' said the ragman.

'See you then,' said Scrumper.

Victoria found herself alone with Scrumper and the wrecked van. 'What do we do now?' she asked.

'Dunno. 'Spect all Hameed's money went on the van. Now just look at it.'

'I wonder . . .' began Victoria with a far away look in her eyes. 'I wonder if my little friend could put it right again?'

'Oh great! Has he got a workshop, your friend?'

'No – no, just a few magic tricks,' replied Victoria.

Scrumper looked at her and began to wind an imaginary handle at the side of his head. 'You're worse than I am,' he said. 'But go on, tell me more.'

'Let's see. On Wednesdays he goes up Strawberry Hill way. He's very fond of strawberries you see.'

'Didn't know strawberries grew on Strawberry Hill,' said Scrumper with a puzzled look.

'No, of course they don't. There aren't any real strawberries there. My friend walks up and down sniffing and using his imagination.'

Scrumper took a few paces away from Victoria and looked her up and down to see if she was serious. She was, because she went on: 'Mondays and Thursdays he goes to Primrose Hill. He's very fond of primroses.'

'That's right,' interrupted Scrumper. 'He sniffs and uses his imagination.'

'Yes, then on Tuesdays and Sundays it's Lavender Hill. . . .'

'Don't tell me,' laughed Scrumper. 'He's fond of lavender too.'

'Of course,' said Victoria simply. 'Who isn't?'

'What about Fridays and Saturdays?' urged Scrumper.

'Oh, nothing in particular on those days. Just whatever takes his fancy. Today's Saturday, so he could be anywhere.'

'That's easy then,' said Scrumper. 'All we have to do is look – anywhere!' He was beginning to like Victoria more and more. She was so full of surprises and not like any other girl he had ever met.

80

'Come on, let's go. You get in the pram and I'll push you.'

Victoria climbed in and they set off to find the Rapid Restorer. Over the dusty ground they trundled, coughing and spluttering, and Scrumper guided the pushpam through a churchyard which he said was a short-cut to the main road. As they passed through the leafy coolness, Scrumper pointed between the trees to what looked like a very tall thin tombstone: 'What's that? It looks like Cleopatra's Needle, but it can't be, not here.'

'No, it certainly isn't!' shouted Victoria excitedly. 'It's my friend. Yoo-hoo!' she called, leaping out of the pushpam and running across the grass. 'You're wonderful! You always seem to be in the right place at the right time. How do you do it?'

'Good day, Miss Plumb,' said the little creature who was sitting cross-legged on the grass. 'All I know is that it's the right time and the right place for mending holes in pockets. I always do it here. So peaceful you know.'

He was stitching one of the many pockets in his bright yellow bolero, using a minute needle and transparent thread. 'I've done fifteen pockets already and this one is almost finished. I have a sewing day once every year. Oh!' he said, suddenly noticing Scrumper. 'You've got a friend with you.'

Victoria had forgotten about Scrumper for a moment. 'Yes,' she said. 'This is Scrumper Flint. He's a VERY GOOD friend of mine.' She said this with a special smile that seemed to please the boy. 'We've been looking for you. Something dreadful's happened to Hameed's tea stall. It ran away and got wrecked. I wondered if you could help.'

'Hameed's tea stall? Mm, I doubt it,' said the Rapid Restorer slipping on his bolero, and pushing his repair kit into one of his furry boots. 'I never tamper with mechanical things.'

'Well, you couldn't call it mechanical any more, sir,' said Scrumper, polite for the first time in his life. 'It's more like a dead wreck.'

'For Victoria, I will try anything once,' said the little fellow with a wide smile. 'Take me to it.'

'If you can both get in the pushpam, we'll get back all the quicker,' said Scrumper gallantly. But, with his pile of hats and his sandwich-board, the Rapid Restorer couldn't actually fit in, so he sat at the front with his legs dangling. Scrumper had difficulty in steering with his face almost pressed against the sandwich-board, but he adjusted the side mirrors like all good drivers, so that at least he could see where he had come from.

He followed the sloping land and it brought him back to the rag and bone yard. The blue van was still there, looking very squashed indeed. The windows were broken, the counter was split in half, and one of the doors was hanging on a bent hinge.

The Rapid Restorer looked it over, rubbing his chin. 'You do find me some hard tasks, Miss Plumb,' he said. 'And I haven't been within sniffing distance of a pancake since I last saw you. What's the outlook in that direction?'

'Poor. Very poor I'm afraid. All the food's been ruined, and anyway what's left is in the ragman's dustbin now.'

Scrumper's eyes twinkled and he jumped into the van. There he found half a currant bun stuck to the roof by its butter. 'How's this?' he asked, jumping out again.

'Thank you young man, I'll try.' The Rapid Restorer took a bite, and although he didn't seem to like the taste, he managed to swallow it. Then he prepared to do his magic trick by first pulling his pockets inside-out, but Victoria found to her horror that she couldn't stand on her head. She tried harder than she had ever tried before, but she couldn't do it. Each time she turned upside-down, she collapsed on the ground.

'It's no use. I can't do it today,' she admitted miserably. 'It must be the excitement or something. Could you manage without me for once?'

'Impossible! Disastrous! I've come to rely on your help you see. We must expect failure.' The Rapid Restorer closed his eyes and began his heel-and-toe dance. It wasn't as lively as usual, and Victoria felt ashamed as she stood by and watched. She looked at Scrumper, but he whispered: 'Don't look at me. My head's the wrong shape.'

The dance went on and on, but the blue van remained the same. After fully four minutes, the Rapid Restorer seemed to be tiring. His heels and toes were not working at the usual speed. 'I have a distinct feeling that nothing is happening,' he said, without opening his eyes. 'Am I right?'

'That's it,' said Scrumper. 'It's as mangled as ever. Now what do we do?'

'No, no! Wait a minute,' cried Victoria excitedly. A change was taking place at the back of the van. It was like the mixing of a television picture. The damaged part of the van was disappearing and at the same time it was reappearing like a brand new vehicle. At least the back part was doing that, but the front was vanishing and not coming back at all! 'It's – well, it's only half there. The front half's gone altogether. Will it come back, do you think?'

The Rapid Restorer opened his eyes and shook his head: 'Most unlikely. It should be here by now, if it's coming at all. Sorry, but the currant bun was not a pancake, and your head was not in order, Miss Plumb.'

They asked him if he would try again, but he would not in case something worse happened. 'Disappointment for all,' he said. 'But it is better than nothing. Now I must get back to my sixteenth pocket. I have forty-seven to do altogether.' He waved goodbye and walked away with astonishing speed until he was gone from sight.

'But how strong is his magic?' asked Scrumper looking at the van. 'I mean, it's standing on two wheels. There aren't any front ones. What happens if the magic doesn't last?'

'It will fall down!' said Victoria. They looked at each other for a second, then both made a sudden dash to collect stones and bricks to prop up the van. When they had made it secure, Victoria thoughtfully took the money out of the till in case it should be stolen. She made a note of it and gave the money to Scrumper to take care of, showing how much she trusted him. After that, they went home.

The summer holidays had begun when Victoria went back one day to find the tea stall still in the same place and still propped up with the front half missing. Hameed was hobbling up and down outside it with his leg in plaster, while Scrumper was inside serving tea to the ragman from the yard.

' 'Ere she comes at last,' cried Scrumper. 'Wotcher Vicky! Sorry, hello Victoria.'

Victoria replied with three cartwheels which brought her exactly to Hameed's plaster cast. 'Sorry I couldn't come sooner,' she said. 'I had to help Mum wallpaper the staircase. She won't get on a ladder unless I'm holding on to it. How's business?'

'Only good when Scrumper comes,' sighed Hameed, slapping his crutches. 'He is a good boy, and I am useless.'

'Yes, but worst luck my mum and dad are taking me to Southend for two weeks, and we don't know what to do here,' said Scrumper glumly.

'That's all right,' said Victoria brightly. 'You go to Southend, and I'll help Hameed.'

But Scrumper shook his head. 'No, you live too far off, and it's not the place for a girl, stuck out here with all the money. Too dangerous!'

It was then that the ragman spoke. 'I'm on the road most days, else I'd help,' he said in a voice that sounded more like a wheeze. 'Tell you what though, I'll scout around if you like.'

'You are kindness itself,' said Hameed gratefully.

'Think nothing of it mate,' said the ragman, looking embarrassed that someone should feel grateful to him. 'Takes liquorice allsorts to make a world, as the saying goes.'

Victoria's mind was working faster than usual. She always thought quicker after a few cartwheels. She was thinking particularly of noses. The ragman's nose was long enough for a badger, let alone a rag-picker. She thought of other noses – long noses – noses like elephants. The Dowsers! Sir Partridge and Lady Dowser! Those two grand old people who had been so kind to her once when she had banged her head on their car, the First Choice Roaster. She turned impulsively to the ragman. 'Mr . . . er Mr . . . er. . . .'

'Kronk!' said the ragman apologetically. 'Sorry about that. Kronk's the name – Matthew Kronk, or Kronkers as some people likes to call me.'

'Yes Mr Konker – Konk er . . . Kronk,' stammered Victoria. 'I was wondering, do you ever go anywhere near Eatwell Place?'

Mr Kronk's eyes lit up as though they had been switched on. 'I should jolly say so! My second home that is, Eatwell Place. Folks up there throw out stuff fit for a palace, they do. Too much money and no sense, says I.'

'Two friends of mine live there,' announced Victoria grandly. Mr Kronk gave her a disbelieving look. 'Honest,' went on Victoria, 'at number forty-three – a Sir and a Lady.'

'Number forty-three! I knows it. Nobody's lived there for years. Empty as a hole that one.'

'Well, they were there last autumn, because my friend – oh, never mind. Would you give me a lift next time you're going up there, please? I've got business that's very important.'

'So now's the time, right this minute. Off we pop! Nobody ever says old Kronk's not obliging.' He put his fingers to his lips and whistled: 'Wheeee! Cissy-belle? Show a leg then!'

Scrumper and Victoria both expected Mrs Kronk to appear, if there was one, but from the cobblestone yard came the dainty clip-clop of hooves gathering speed. Out through the gateway came the ragman's brown and white horse, pulling the red cart which had been repaired. Freshly hand-painted flowers were glowing brightly round the sides.

'Hooray!' shouted Victoria jumping up and down. 'I think I might be able to help you, Hameed. I won't be long. See you later Scrumper.'

'I suppose you know what you're doing, because I don't,' called Scrumper. Mr Kronk lifted Victoria up into the driver's wooden seat and climbed up beside her. With a gentle flick of the reins away went Cissy-belle tossing her mane with delight. 'Eatwell Place, my beauty,' said Kronk who clearly was very fond of his horse. 'Understands every word I say, so she does. Just like a dog,' he said.

It was the most thrilling ride of Victoria's life. The wind whistled through her ears with a sound like the sea, and when they went over Vauxhall Bridge, she thought the cross-wind would lift her clean out of the cart. She hung on to Kronk's arm until they got to the other side, and her tummy was still fluttering when they turned into Eatwell Place. They stopped in front of number forty-three. 'Like I told you – empty, see?' said Kronk.

'No, it can't be,' said Victoria. 'Isn't that a bottle of milk on the doorstep?'

'Well, wipe my blinkers, so it is by the looks of things. Always thought it was empty, I did,' said Mr Kronk, scratching his head.

'I'm going to ring the bell,' said Victoria, leaping out of the cart. She had just reached the top step when the door slowly opened and Lady Dragora stood there in her lace dress and pearls, just as Victoria remembered her.

'Oh, so sorry, I thought it was Sir Partridge,' she said in surprise. 'I'm afraid we're not officially at home today. I hope you will forgive me.'

'Oh, that's all right,' said Victoria. 'Don't you remember me? Victoria Plumb. I banged my head on your car last Christmas, and my friend put your house up again after it had been knocked down.'

'Ah, but of course I remember. How nice of you to call. D'you know we haven't been knocked down again, I'm glad to say. We were told later it had all been a mistake.'

Just then there was a squeaking and a groaning as the First Choice Roaster drew up at the pavement. Out came Sir Partridge carrying two bags of potato crisps. 'Lunch is up, my sweetheart,' he announced, before he noticed Victoria. 'Oh, I say now if it isn't the little Plumb girl. Good-day, it IS good to see you.'

'I really came to ask if you could help a friend of mine,' said Victoria. 'He's broken his leg, and there's no one to take over his tea stall. I couldn't think of anyone else to ask.'

'Tea stall? Tea stall, eh? That sounds interesting,' said Sir Partridge. 'What do you say Draggy? We've gone and lost our news-round, you know. The dashed newsagent's been demolished! Everything's going! The world's coming to an end. The Armada's at it again. Have a crisp, Victoria,' he said generously, tearing open one of the bags. 'Salt and vinegar flavour. Answer me, old girl. Do you fancy a tea stall, eh?'

'Oh good gracious, I'm not sure, Partridge,' said Lady Dragora. 'Where is it exactly?'

Victoria bent down and picked up the bottle of milk as she tried to think what to say. 'Well, it's in a kind of area, but it will be somewhere when the buildings go up,' she muttered. All she could really think of was that it was somewhere in the desert.

'What does it matter where it is,' said Sir Partridge, with a mouthful of crisps. 'We're down to our last copper, that's all I know. Of course we'll do it. Couldn't be more suitable. Tell your friend he can count on the Dowsers.'

'Hooray! Hooray!' shouted Victoria for the second time that day. And she gave each of the Dowsers a hug and a kiss. 'Mr Kronk, Mr Kronk, it's all settled,' she called out.

Mr Kronk smiled from his perch on the cart. 'Great that is, just great. My Cissy-belle's getting fidgety, are you coming?'

Victoria leapt down the steps, discovered she was still clutching the pint of milk and leapt up again. She gave the milk to Lady Dragora, then with a sudden brainwave she whisked herself upside down and walked out to the cart on her hands. The Dowsers and Kronk clapped their hands, so to finish off the exercise, she did a cartwheel right beside – the cartwheel, and bounced up into the seat without any help from the ragman.

'I'll come back when I've told Hameed the good news,' she said happily to the elderly couple who were smiling broadly.

And that's how it was settled. Just as simply as that. Each day, good old Kronk crossed the river and brought Sir Partridge and Lady Dragora down to manage the tea stall, until Hameed's leg was

better. They thoroughly enjoyed themselves. Sir Partridge had been out in India in his youth, and nothing suited him better than a cup of excellent Indian tea. And, as Lady Dragora frequently said: 'We do meet such interesting people now, Partridge.'

Victoria was happy for all of them, and she marvelled at the number of good friends she had made in the space of twelve months.

Two Ripe Old Plumbs

Victoria had been given a pair of roller skates for her birthday, in the autumn, because that's what she had wanted. Really, she wanted a dog, but Mrs Plumb said that was out of the question. No dog, no stray cat – a stray pram was the most she was willing to put up with because at least it was useful.

'I should have called you Victor,' her mother shouted over the gate one day, as she dried her hands on her apron. 'You're more like a boy than a girl. Can't think what you'll grow up into – not a lady, that's for sure.'

Victoria gave her mother a huge smile as she skimmed past the gate, with pigtails flying and arms swinging from left to right. 'Come on Mum,' she laughed. 'Have a go! It'll put a spring in your step!'

'I beg your pardon!' said Mrs Plumb, vanishing into the house, quickly. She always said that when she couldn't think of a better reply. But she peeped at Victoria through the curtains, and smiled secretly, admiring the way her daughter had taught herself to skate beautifully in only five days. 'Skates was a good idea after all,' she murmured to herself. 'At least they stop her from standing on her head, until the day of course when she learns to skate on her head.'

As she watched, she saw Victoria waving happily to someone along the avenue. Out she went to look, naturally. Nothing was ever allowed to escape Mrs Plumb's notice, if she could help it.

It was Granny and Grandpa Plumb, shuffling along arm in arm, and looking as though they were desperately trying to hurry. When they saw Mrs Plumb, Grandpa took off his cloth cap and waved it in the air, urgently. 'We've got to go! We've got to go,' he called, in a creaking, high old way.

'Where, Grandpa? Where have you got to go?' asked Victoria, scooping to a stop beside them.

'Down. We've – we've all got to go down,' panted Grandpa Plumb. By this time, they had reached the gate.

'You mean Russell Terrace is coming down after all?' asked Mrs Plumb, drying her hands on her apron again, for no reason.

'Yes, they mean business this time,' sighed Granny Plumb, stepping into the house. 'Oh, quick Ethel, a cup of tea before we pass out.' She dropped with a loud 'twang' into Mr Plumb's old armchair, and pulled a piece of paper from her handbag. 'Look, it's all here in black and white. Our last chance to get out.'

'What? Your foundations taken from under your

very feet, just because somebody says so? My George was born in that house. Some people have a nerve!' said Mrs Plumb with her mouth opening and shutting in her really-shocked way.

It was true that Russell Terrace, a street about ten minutes' walk from Backfire Avenue, was due to be rebuilt. All the houses in the terrace had been emptied and boarded up, all except the Plumbs' house. They had refused to leave. Now it seemed they would have to, or be demolished when the terrace was torn apart.

'Lived there all our married lives, we have.' Poor Granny Plumb was so upset there were tears in her eyes. 'We'll be parted now, and we were so close. I don't know where they'll put us.'

' 'Spect they'll give us a tent nearby, if we're lucky. I think I saw one on the pavement,' laughed Grandpa, trying to cheer her up, but this made her cry more than ever.

'Oh! Oh! I couldn't live in a tent, not at my age. Not even for one night, I couldn't,' she cried bitterly. Mrs Plumb ran to put the kettle on and tried to pop a digestive biscuit into Granny's mouth, as if it might stop the tears.

Victoria had heard all this from the open front door, and was gone as fast as her skates could take her, round to Russell Terrace. Her grandparents lived at number six, the house in the middle. She went there at least twice a week to do errands and a bit of weeding and she loved to pick scented sweet-peas there in the summertime. Victoria always thought it was like going into the country because there were three apple trees and a lilac in the big back garden. But it was all going to disappear. The Demon Demolition Gang already had their machinery parked there, and on the pavement was a red-and-white striped tent, the one Grandpa had joked about.

As Victoria skated past, the zip on the tent was pulled open a little and a voice said: 'Psst! Psst!' Was it the Demon Demolition Gang lying in wait? Slowly Victoria approached and peeped under the flap. No! It was the Rapid Restorer!

'Corks!! I was just wondering about you. Did you know about it then?' she asked, crouching down.

'Of course. Who doesn't? Plain for weeks. It will happen soon. Sssh! Not a word about me.'

'How are you off for pan . . .' Victoria began, but the zip was smartly closed.

'Supply in readiness, thank you Miss Plumb. You were enjoying your skates so much, I didn't like to trouble you,' came the little voice from within.

Victoria skated up and down as quietly as she could, looking for the Demon Demolition Gang, but they were not to be seen. It was then that Granny and Grandpa Plumb turned into Russell Terrace, with Mrs Plumb, who was glowering at all the houses, especially the few on the other side that were not going to be pulled down.

'You have a sit-in,' she was saying. 'Don't budge. Not an inch. Leave it all to me. You'll get every-thing you need, then we'll soon see if they dare pull your house down about your ears.'

This started Granny Plumb crying all over again. 'What, all down on the top of us? Oh, Ethel.'

Then Mrs Plumb's eyes alighted on the striped tent. 'Look! They're at it already, disconnecting your phone. I'll disconnect his. . . .' She was about to unzip the tent and do something terrible to whoever was inside, when Victoria quickly blocked her way.

'No, Mum, no! Grandpa hasn't got a telephone, remember?' she said – just in time.

'Oh, neither he has.' Mrs Plumb was disappointed that she could not do something dramatic. 'Well anyway, let's get both of you inside, and inside you stay. Bolt every bolt. Bar every bar. Remember now, don't give in, just stay in!'

So that is what happened. The elderly Plumbs locked and barricaded themselves in and vowed not to give in and not to come out. Mrs Plumb had a brainwave of sending food up on a pulley system. She said she had seen this sort of a thing done somewhere before. Victoria smiled quietly, remembering the pulley for the pushpam, and the crash landing. Yes, her mother had seen something like it before.

The next day, the Demon Demolition Gang were on the job. Tosher, Fruity and Plonker, looking mightier and fiercer than ever, started work on the nine empty houses. Within a few days, only the old Plumbs' house was left. It stood all alone among the wreckage. The Rapid Restorer waited silently in his tent while his supply of pancakes became stale.

Mrs Plumb practically lived on the doorstep. Mr Plumb often found his dinner at home in the oven, and Victoria whizzed about on her skates after school, keeping up the supplies. She had mastered the art of skating and pushpaming at the same time, and her mother was beginning to think she had a genius in the family. She called it our Plumb's Express Delivery Service, and sometimes sent out for an odd packet of this or that, for the sheer thrill of the speed at which it came.

Now that all the houses were down except one, the Demon Demolition Gang were tired of sitting about eating hot dogs and chewing their gum. But they brightened up on the fourth day when a man from the council rode up on a bicycle. He wore a raincoat and held a megaphone on one of the handlebars. He parked his bicycle, carefully took the bicycle clips from his trousers and called through the megaphone:

'Can you hear me, Mr and Mrs Plumb?'

'No we can't!' shouted Granny Plumb defiantly, opening the sash window and slamming it down again.

'We'll have no more nonsense,' went on the man. 'Come along now, you be good people and move out like everybody else, before your house falls down. We don't want to be unkind. It's for your own good. What do you say?'

Grandpa Plumb's answer was to pull his old gramophone over to the window and wind the handle. Then he bowed to the few people who had gathered in the street and put on a record. It whined and moaned and squeaked until the song became clear:

> *'My old girl's a Lambeth pearl,*
> *Down the Lane with her barrow in the morning;*
> *Fruit piled high, holding up the sky,*
> *Every day you'll hear her calling:*
> *Ripe bananas! Get your bananas here!*
> *Green, yellow or brown!'*

The council man angrily pulled his raincoat about him, fixed on his bicycle clips and pedalled off to give this reply to the Town Hall. Three times he came back that day, and three times the same song was played to drown his words. The Demon Demolition Gang were prowling about like angry gorillas, but there was nothing they could do until the house was empty.

On the fifth day, Victoria, who had always pretended not to notice the striped tent, again heard a 'Psst! Psst!' She leaned against the tent and the Rapid Restorer whispered through the zip: 'Something must be done quickly. My pancakes are like bricks. I've never worked with stale pancakes before. Listen. House must be demolished, BUT, all rubble must be collected and I will put it up somewhere.'

'I could go for more pancakes?' suggested Victoria.

'No. House is dangerous. If gale comes – disaster.'

'Right. But who . . . ? How . . . ? I know, Matthew Kronk and the Dowsers. They'll help,' whispered Victoria. 'You be getting on with your pancakes while I'm gone.'

Victoria was of course still on her skates. She only took them off to go to school or to bed. So, away she went like rolling lightning to Hameed's tea stall which was still parked by the rag and bone yard. The Dowsers were so happy with the company and good tea that they had stayed on with Hameed even though his leg was quite better.

'Of course we'll come!' said Sir Partridge beaming when he heard the story. 'Life gets more interesting every week. We'll probably manage all the furniture in the First Choice Roaster. It's up at Eatwell Place, but we'll bring it down. Too expensive to drive it every day.'

'And we'd never get here every day if you tried, my love, would we?' put in Lady Dragora. 'But how exciting! Let's do it right away Partridge.'

Hameed had gone to buy sugar and Matthew Kronk was out on his rounds, but the Dowsers promised that everything would be arranged for the next morning, very early.

By this time, the people at the Town Hall were thoroughly tired of the Plumb trouble, and the next morning, extra early, they sent their man back again on his bicycle with a final request. This time he did not dismount, but quickly raised his megaphone and shouted:

'Keep the bananas off and listen to me for once.'

Grandpa Plumb, still in his dressing-gown, raised his cap politely and listened.

'Look, we've got a space near here we don't need for a while. It's on the corner of Flat Iron Row, by Mrs Kelly's paper shop. AND you'll have a little bit of garden, AND you'll be right beside your son

George Plumb in Backfire Avenue. That's our final offer. Now what do you say?'

Grandpa Plumb's answer came quick as a flash: 'We'd rather have a couple of rooms at Buckingham Palace, but if that's the best you can do, we'll take it.'

But Victoria wasn't satisfied. 'My Grandpa will only take it if you don't need that space for a long, long, long time,' she said, thinking quickly as usual.

'We've no plans for that space for the next fifty years, little lady. It will be put in writing, signed and sealed,' said the weary man, whose megaphone was now very battered from wear and tear on his handlebars.

'It's a deal. We'll be packed in a jiffy,' called Granny Plumb, trying to smile.

'And you won't see us for dust,' added Grandpa.

Victoria had already sent secret messages up in the food bucket about the Rapid Restorer's plans. The only thing she had not been sure of was *where* the house could be rebuilt. Now it was settled.

Within a few minutes the Dowsers drove up in their First Choice Roaster and it held every stick of furniture the old Plumbs owned with plenty of space to spare for them as well. They drove round to Flat Iron Row, parked near Mrs Kelly's shop and waited.

Then the real action began. The Demon Demolition Gang were on the scene, livid at being kept waiting. They had the old house down within minutes and were anxious to be on their way. As they passed the striped tent, Tosher gave it a hard slap on the side: 'Having trouble too, mate? You've been 'ere as long as we 'ave!'

'Ur! Urgrurg! Ur!' growled the Rapid Restorer, trying to sound like one of them. They seemed to understand him perfectly, and went away, thumping out of sight.

Matthew Kronk and Cissy-belle soon loomed up in the yellow dust and the bricks and woodwork were lifted on to the cart. It took Cissy-belle many trots back and forth and it was hard work, but like most animals, she was a willing worker and did not complain.

The Rapid Restorer raised his sandwich-board and the striped tent rose with it. For those who watched, it was an odd sight to see a workman's tent moving along the pavement at great speed. A trick of the early morning light in all that choking dust, was probably what most of them thought. Round in Flat Iron Row, Mrs Kelly was too busy in her shop, sorting out her paper-rounds, to know what was going on outside.

What WAS going on was that the Rapid Restorer, with his pockets pulled inside-out, had started to perform his heel-and-toe dance, with Victoria beside him, standing on her head. Up came the house, brick by brick, windows, front door, back door, the next floor, then the roof. But one floor was missing! There had been yet another one in Russell Terrace. The Rapid Restorer said either they had failed to bring all the bricks, or it was caused by his indigestion from eating stale pancakes. But it pleased Granny Plumb. 'That house always had too many stairs. Got on my nerves, it did. This suits me very well. Thanks ever so,' she said, shaking the Rapid Restorer's hand with big jerks. Between them, all the friends helped to carry in the pieces of furniture and other things.

The sky was darkening on that short day in late autumn by the time the Plumbs had put everything in order. That was when there came a loud, honk-honking in the street. A huge trailer was trying to edge past the First Choice Roaster. It had brought the mobile home from the council.

Grandpa opened the front door and stood on the top step. 'Looks like you took a wrong turning. You should be taking that thing north by north-west, not south by south-west. I know all about it,' he said, seriously.

'Quite likely,' replied the man, dully. 'I'm always being sent out on mistakes. Life's like that nowadays.' With Grandpa's help, he reversed along the street and was gone, in the hope of finding an empty corner somewhere north by north-west.

In the meantime, Victoria skated off along Flat Iron Row to find the one person who was missing – the Rapid Restorer. She went right to the cross-roads, but there was no sign of him or the striped tent. 'One day I'll catch him in time,' she thought. 'But no, perhaps that's part of his life, the way he has to be. He's here when he's needed, and gone when the job's done.' As she cruised back, she checked to see if there was already a number six Flat Iron Row, but curiously, all the numbers were odd ones. 'They must have ironed out all the even ones,' she laughed to herself in the darkness.

She expected Granny and Grandpa Plumb to be in bed after all the excitement of the day, but not at all. The corner of the street joining on to Backfire Avenue was buzzing with people dashing about. Old Mrs Kelly, who was about to shut her shop for the night, reopened it and produced packets of biscuits, fruit drinks and an assortment of snacks. Mrs McKnocker was there, flapping tablecloths about, trestle tables were being put up in the middle of the road, and a rope stretched across to stop the traffic. Things seemed to be coming from everywhere. Dozens of sandwiches had been made by Sir Partridge and Lady Dragora, who were now expert at it, and Mrs Plumb was mixing a mountain of instant pudding in a basin. Grandpa Plumb looked very important strutting up and down with his best woollen scarf tucked into his waistcoat, and his real gold watch-chain dangling beside it.

'What's all this?' asked Victoria, whose legs were beginning to ache.

'It's a celebration for what that little friend of yours has done for us. Great fellow, your Rupert Restorer. Let me shake him by the hand,' said Grandpa, looking about.

'Sorry Grandpa. He's gone.'

'Gone? Why? Where is he?'

'Er . . . Well, I think it's past his bedtime, or something. He has to walk as far as the Albert Bridge you know.'

'Too bad,' said Grandpa Plumb, obviously disappointed. 'You bring him along one day Victoria. I want a word with him. I was a brick-layer when I was young, but I could never work as fast as he did.'

Victoria turned to hug her Granny who had just come out of the house wearing her pink newly-knitted, poncho-shawl-cape-thing as she called it. 'Oh Granny, I'm so glad you didn't have to move far away. I think it's important to have Grans and Gramps close by. We'll always be together, won't we?'

'Course we will lovie,' smiled Granny Plumb, at last without the trace of a tear.

'That raincoat chappie said fifty years, didn't he? That should be long enough for us,' laughed Grandpa, hugging Granny and Victoria both at the same time.

While this conversation had been going on, a street party had materialized. There were even coloured lights strung across the street. 'I've never seen anything like this before,' gasped Victoria.

'It's like the end of the last war, which you know nothing about, my girl,' said Mrs Plumb. 'I remember it, but only just. I was in the Land Army, and me terrified at the sight of a live chicken.'

It was a wonderful evening. Cissy-belle was un-harnessed and she cropped all the grass in sight, then ate as many buns as were good for her. Victoria's father arrived at last, late from the laundry, and he had half a dozen tongues telling him all at once what had happened. The night air was cold. With all the autumn leaves having long

since fluttered away, winter seemed to be creeping in, but nobody minded.

Grandpa Plumb suddenly had an idea which he said called for complete silence, even chewing was to be done with mouths closed. He went into number six, opened the window and wound up the gramophone.

'Oh, no! Here come the bananas again,' sighed Granny Plumb, sleepily. But it was not. It was not about bananas at all. It was:

'*There's a shop around the corner with a – thing. Ting! Ting!*
When you climb the steps and walk in, hear it ring. Ting! Ting!
If you think you've lost your pocket,
Mrs Kelly's surely got it,
In her shop around the corner with a – thing. Ting! Ting!'

Front doors opened. Heads looked out of windows and everyone joined in singing so heartily that they did not notice the temperature dropping, not until the first snowflakes of winter settled on their hair, and moistened their sandwiches.

How long it lasted, Victoria did not know. She was thinking of Scrumper and wishing he was with her, instead of being in bed with measles, when she fell asleep with her head on a plate of jelly.

When she woke in the morning, she knew it had really happened because she saw in the mirror that there were blobs of red jelly on her face. She looked out of her bedroom window. Snow had fallen heavily during the night. The grubby street was covered up. It was pure and white, like a lovely new world, waiting to be wakened up and lived in. A tiny puff of a breeze blew and a paper napkin fluttered by. It told her that Granny and Grandpa Plumb were very near, just around the corner.

Victoria climbed happily back into bed, without knowing that it was not red jelly on her face – but measles! She was sharing measles with Scrumper, just as they shared everything else.

In a day or two, he came to see her, and when she told him about number six Flat Iron Row, he was as happy as she was. You see, Scrumper had no granny or grandpa, but it was not long before he truly felt that he had.

Jubilation Day

One morning, Mrs Plumb woke up around six-thirty and leapt out of bed so swiftly, she hit the bedside table. The sudden leap was because the alarm clock had not rung. Its sound reassured her every morning that it was time to get up, but on this particular morning it had not rung at all, so she was quite lost.

'George! George!' she called, groping about like a sleep-walker. 'The clock didn't ring. Get up quickly. You'll be late for the laundry. You'll get the sack, George!'

She pushed and pulled at Mr Plumb who refused to be wakened. As she pulled off the covers, so he pulled them back up again. 'Numph!' was what he seemed to be saying, as he stuffed his head under his pillow.

'George Plumb! If you lose your job and your pension, and we die of starvation, I'll – I'll never forgive you – never.' Mrs Plumb was yelling loud enough to waken the whole of Backfire Avenue. Mr Plumb knew the only way to stop it was to sit up, so he did.

'Ethel,' he said, with one eye open. 'My ever-lasting Ethel! It's a National Holiday. Now will you come back to bed and keep quiet.'

This had no effect on Mrs Plumb at all. 'You're not with the National, you're with the Snowhite laundry. Get into your socks, and be quick about it.' She was on her knees, trying frantically to push her husband's toes into his socks, when Victoria's sleepy head appeared in the doorway.

'Dad means it's Jubilation Day,' said Victoria helpfully, but she said it in the middle of such a wide yawn that her mother understood nothing.

'Back to bed, Victoria. You're too early, and your Dad's too late. One and a half hours yet before porridge time, so off you go. And, as for you George Plumb, your eggs and bacon will be ready in fifteen minutes exactly, or you'll have to go off hungry. It's entirely up to you!'

Mrs Plumb pulled on her dressing-gown and slippers, and shuffled down to the kitchen, thinking how fortunate that there was at least one responsible

person in the household. She had got herself into such a dither, tussling with her husband's socks and feet, that her curlers were hanging round her head like pink plastic ringlets.

'Don't know why he has to have a cooked breakfast anyway,' she grumbled, as she cooked the bacon. 'It can't be good for him, jogging it all up and down in that laundry van.'

She was still complaining to herself when she reached for the tea caddy – the tea caddy she had used for years and years. She had almost reached the shelf, when her hand stopped in mid-air. It was a lovely tea caddy, decorated with a picture of a coronation.

'Coronation!' she whispered. 'Funny? That rings a bell.' She made the tea and went on repeating softly: 'Coronation. Coronation.'

All this was seen and heard by Victoria, who had not gone back to bed but was standing on her head in the corner of the sitting-room. She knew her mother would sort herself out, but in the meantime it was hard to keep still and not to laugh.

'Coronation! Jubilation! National Holiday!' went on Mrs Plumb, cracking eggs almost by the half dozen. 'Snowhite L. . . .'

'And the seven dwarfs!' screeched Victoria, who couldn't stand still a moment longer. 'It's Dad's day off. He told you ages ago.' She rolled about the carpet like a pink and white striped ball in her pyjamas, and couldn't stop laughing.

'Oh, Victoria, you silly girl. You might have told me properly,' said her mother, climbing over her and going to the bottom of the stairs. 'GEORGE? You can take your socks off and go back to sleep. It's a National Holiday.' She called this as though she was announcing the latest news. Mr Plumb did not reply.

Victoria was still making a fiendish racket on the carpet. She thought it was getting funnier and funnier. But her mother was of a different opinion. 'Enough's enough, Victoria. How am I supposed to remember these things all the year round, just tell me that?'

Victoria stood up and tried to straighten her face. 'But, Mum, it doesn't happen all the year round – not even once a year. This happens after twenty-five years!'

'Then that makes it all the more difficult to remember, doesn't it? Come on, let's go back to bed. I'm very sorry. It's all my fault. I'll apologize all round.'

But at that moment Mr Plumb appeared, fully dressed. 'Well, you got us up, so here we are Ethel. My, that bacon smells good.'

'Sorry George. I got all of a flutter. I thought. . . .' Mrs Plumb went back to preparing the breakfast.

Her husband patted her on the shoulder and plonked her bedraggled plastic curlers. 'Never mind Ethel. We all make mistakes, and this might have been a good idea of yours. With an early breakfast inside us, we can be sure of getting a good viewing place.'

Mrs Plumb was about to take a bite of toast: 'A good viewing place? What do you mean George?

There are only three of us. We don't usually have to fight for viewing space. It is a twenty-six inch screen, isn't it?'

'I'm not talking about the television, Ethel. We're going out to see the real thing. It's the only one of its kind we'll see in our life-time.'

'OUT? When we can see it in comfort at home?' Mrs Plumb was so amazed, she put down her knife and fork.

'OUT!' repeated Mr Plumb, who was usually very easy-going. 'Victoria's going to see it all in colour, in movement, close up, so that she'll remember it for the rest of her life.'

'She can see it, all in colour, in movement and close up, all here on the telly, George Plumb. Are you sure you're awake yet?'

Mr Plumb felt defeated, but only for a moment, until he saw Victoria tapping the side of her nose. 'Then she'll get the smell of it too, and she won't get that at home, will she?' he said firmly.

'Great, Dad! I want to go,' cried Victoria. 'Let's be there first, right in the front row, and don't forget your camera. Can Scrumper come with us? Can I go and see?'

'Of course he can come, if he wants to. But remember he may not be up yet.'

Victoria was going to see anyway, so she dressed quickly and was about to dash out when her mother called: 'Ask Granny and Grandpa Plumb to come and see it here in colour. Somebody might as well make use of it, otherwise the robbers will have it while we're out.'

It was surprising how many people were up early that morning. Scrumper was pleased to be asked because, like Mrs Plumb, his parents wanted to watch it at home. Victoria then scorched round to the elderly Plumbs who said they'd be there, on the dot.

Mrs Plumb refused to dress up for the occasion. 'My old shopping clothes are good enough,' she said, still casting looks at the television set. 'There's no use wearing my flower-petal hat to be jostled by crowds, trampled by horses or even rolled over by carriages.' She wore her raincoat, although it promised to be a hot day, and tied a headscarf under her chin. It was patterned with dogs.

'That should please somebody,' whispered Victoria to Scrumper, who had just arrived and had the presence of mind to bring a periscope with him.

Sandwiches were hastily prepared, a few apples thrown into a bag, and they were ready to go, just as Granny and Grandpa Plumb came to the door, armed with nuts, potato crisps and a box of chocolates. 'Looks like you're having a Jubilee celebration too then,' said Mrs Plumb, wishing all the more that she could stay at home.

'I should say so,' creaked Granny Plumb. 'A colour telly needs a bit of style to go with it.'

'That's it,' agreed Grandpa Plumb. 'Our old black and white nods off whenever it feels like it. Just like us, ha, ha!'

As they took their leave, Mr Plumb announced: 'Whitehall's the place for us. We'll catch a bus, then let nature take its course.'

'What does that mean, Dad?' asked Victoria.

'It means, my own dear Queen Victoria, that I hope it doesn't rain and spoil everything. But, if it does, we will suffer it for our Queen and country.'

They headed for the nearest bus stop, with Mrs Plumb trailing behind, reluctantly. The queue they joined was longer than they could have imagined, and the bus did not even take them as far as Whitehall. It was re-routed, so they had to walk the rest of the way. Crowds of people had gathered in Whitehall. Hundreds had already staked their viewing places.

'Where's the fine place at the front for us, George?' demanded Mrs Plumb. 'We won't even see the tip of the busbies from here.'

'Bearskins, not busbies,' corrected Mr Plumb patiently, looking about.

'I don't care what you call them, I just want to see the Queen and her Jubilation,' said Mrs Plumb. She was softening up a little. The decorated streets pleased her and she was fond of her Queen, although she only let it show at moments like this.

Suddenly there was cheering, deafening cheering; the sound of music; the clip-clop of horses' hooves. The ground seemed to be heaving with excitement. Scrumper tried his periscope, but he wasn't tall enough to see anything. Neither was Victoria when she tried it. They were going to see nothing after all.

Mrs Plumb was almost in tears. 'George Plumb, I can't see a thing. I shall just die on this very spot if I miss everything. You made us come, so what are you going to do about it?' She was very upset, so her husband gallantly hoisted her up on to his shoulders. It was fortunate he was used to carrying heavy laundry bags. Mrs Plumb didn't seem to weigh more than several hefty blanket-loads.

'Give Dad the periscope Scrumper, quick,' said Victoria, tugging at his sleeve. 'At least he can use it.' Scrumper did as he was asked. Mrs Plumb was radiant now, perched high on her husband's shoulder. She could see everything and was waving a flag someone had thrust into her hand. And Mr Plumb was tall enough to use the periscope. They were both happy, and seemed to forget about the children.

Victoria was looking at something else. 'Look Scrumper, quick – over there.' She pointed to a tall board that was draped with a Union Jack and as the flag flapped up and down, Victoria and Scrumper just had time to read:

THE RAPID RESTORER

BUILDINGS A SPECIALITY
WHAT'S COME DOWN, CAN GO UP
THE PROOF OF THE PUDDING'S IN THE
EATING

'How does he do it?' shouted Scrumper in all the noise. 'He's always in the right place at the right time.'

They eased their way through the crowds, as only children can, and were soon beside the sandwich-board. The Rapid Restorer was crouching inside. 'Thought you might need me. Hurry now, here comes the procession. Climb up my hats. They're as safe as the Houses of Parliament or Westminster Abbey.' He leaned sideways a little so that Victoria and Scrumper could clamber upwards. Higher and higher they went, holding on to the hats until they were sitting right at the top of the sandwich-board.

There they perched in what seemed like a place of honour, and as the procession came into view, they saw everything as clearly as if they had been in the front row. They saw the reds and the blacks, the yellows and the blues, the gold and the silver; the full glory of it all.

As the special coach and carriages came close, Victoria had a sudden inspiration. She whisked herself upside-down and stood on her hands ON THE NARROW TOP EDGE OF THE SANDWICH-BOARD! Scrumper was proud of her, but he sat tight, where he belonged.

What they both agreed upon afterwards and what thrilled them most of all was that they were sure they got a special smile and a special wave from a white-gloved hand. It seemed somehow very special.

When it was all over, like a passing dream, Victoria and Scrumper slid down to the ground. The Rapid Restorer tucked his flag into his bolero and said he must go as fast as possible to Canterbury. 'Special work waiting. Very important.' And he was gone as usual at speed, in spite of the crowds. 'Thanks for coming, just when you were needed,' Victoria called after him – wherever he was.

The two children rejoined Mr and Mrs Plumb. They couldn't get a bus or a taxi and walked all the way back to Sockwell, yet it didn't seem far at all. Mrs Plumb was in a trance. She said she had never seen anything like it in her life, and she a Londoner born and bred! 'It's all so different in the flesh, isn't it?' she said. 'I'll remember it all my life, and me in my old raincoat and pekinese scarf!'

'I'll remember it too,' laughed Mr Plumb. 'On account of being wrestled into my socks this morning, when every decent owl was asleep.' He wanted to joke about it, because he too felt very, very moved by the occasion.

When they reached Backfire Avenue, Granny and Grandpa Plumb had eaten all their nuts, crisps and chocolates, and cried out excitedly: 'We saw you on the telly, we did! You Ethel, sitting up there like Cleopatra on her needle, and George like Nelson with his telescope. And we saw you Scrumper, and of course Victoria upside-down as usual. You're a right little Plumb, you are!'

'Is that all you remember seeing?' asked Mrs Plumb, untying her headscarf. 'You can see us any day of the week. WE saw THEM! All of them, in the flesh. It was glorious!'

After several cups of tea and lots of chatter, Scrumper and the elderly Plumbs were taken safely home by Mr Plumb. Victoria went happily to bed, and dreamt she was Queen Victoria.

Before Mrs Plumb went to bed, she looked at the coronation tea caddy in the kitchen, and said to it: 'Next time the clock doesn't ring, I'll wait for

George to get up first. Who knows what it might be for next time? I wonder . . . ?'

Humming a well-known anthem to herself, she wearily climbed the stairs, and as she drew the bedroom curtains, her eyes were shining. They shone, reflecting all the silver that glittered from that extra special night sky.

And so, the great Jubilation Day quietly came to a close.